AMY CARMICHAEL

'Beauty for Ashes'

A Biography

By the same author:

The Life of Martyn Lloyd-Jones, 1899–1981
Archibald G. Brown: Spurgeon's Successor
John MacArthur: Servant of the Word and Flock
The Old Evangelicalism

AMY CARMICHAEL

'Beauty for Ashes'

A Biography

Iain H. Murray

THE BANNER OF TRUTH TRUST

THE BANNER OF TRUTH TRUST
3 Murrayfield Road, Edinburgh EH12 6EL, UK
P.O. Box 621, Carlisle, PA 17013, USA

*

© Iain H. Murray, 2015
First published 2015
Reprinted 2015
Reprinted 2015 (special)
Reprinted 2017

ISBN:
Print: 978 1 84871 552 3
EPUB: 978 1 84871 553 0
Kindle: 978 1 84871 554 7

*

Typeset in 11.5/16 pt Sabon Oldstyle Figures at the
Banner of Truth Trust, Edinburgh
Printed in the USA by
Versa Press, Inc.,
East Peoria, IL

**With thankfulness for
The Dohnavur Fellowship**

*To give unto them beauty for ashes, the oil of joy
for mourning, the garment of praise for the spirit
of heaviness; that they might be called trees of
righteousness, the planting of the LORD,
that he might be glorified.*
ISAIAH 61:3

*Suffer little children, and
forbid them not, to come unto me:
for of such is the kingdom of heaven.*
MATTHEW 19:14

CONTENTS

1. Resting on the way to the forest.

ILLUSTRATIONS

Acknowledgements

The publisher is grateful to the Dohnavur Fellowship for use of illustrations 5, 7, 8, 11, 12, 13, 14, 15, 16; Mr Paul Williams for the use of his photographs, 17, 18, 19, 20, and Dr Jacky Woolcock for supplying photograph 21.

FOREWORD

The truly moving biographies of noble Christians are surely encouraging, while also being convicting. They tear at the fabric of our complacency and selfishness. The lifelong sacrificial usefulness of Amy Carmichael fits that pattern. Women today who, in seeking spiritual examples to follow, read the story of Amy will face their own shortcomings and love of comfort.

Iain Murray says: 'It is compulsive writing that leads to compulsive reading.' I might add that a compulsive life begins that sequence. If Amy was anything, she was compelled to love and serve her Lord for His glory.

For all women and men (my husband, John, was first to read this account) who experience this journey to a faraway time and place, my prayer is that it will lift them up and out of the infectious influence of worldly culture that dominates our day.

PATRICIA MACARTHUR
Warmsprings
Santa Clarita
California
November 2014

PREFACE

International tensions can re-route flight paths as happened to me earlier this year. Instead of flying the usual London to Australia route, via Bangkok, our Qantas flight stopped at Dubai, then down over India, before leaving the sub-continent at Cape Comorin, its southern extremity. Thirty miles north of that Cape, our unexpected flight was too high to see anything of a place of which I knew by repute. There, at the beginning of the twentieth century, a Christian oasis came into being of greater power than all India's ancient heathenism. In the Old Testament a promise of divine blessing was expressed in the words, 'the streets shall be full of boys and girls playing'. Something like that happened at Dohnavur in the century after 1901. One thousand eight hundred and fifty girls and six hundred and seventy boys became part of a new family. In addition to playing, there was the love and the Bible teaching which changed lives and prepared witnesses for Jesus Christ. 'A little one shall become a thousand' is a promise fulfilled in Christian history (Isa. 60:22).

I was not always interested in Dohnavur. For one thing, I thought it was only past history. I did not know that after Britain's close tie with India ended in 1947, this work of grace was going on to the present day. For another, I thought that the books of Amy Carmichael, the founder of Dohnavur, would be principally beneficial to Christian women. I was late in discovering my mistake. Not only are her writings a significant part of missionary history, they show how female authors can be at the forefront of devotional evangelical literature, just as they are at the forefront of hymnody devoted to the person of Christ.

I have sought to put these pages together not out of penitence but rather out of the sheer enjoyment and profit which has been involved. Amy Carmichael is one of the best-recorded evangelicals of the twentieth century, and her two leading biographies, Frank Houghton's *Amy Carmichael of Dohnavur* and Elisabeth Elliot's *A Chance to Die*, continue to be currently available. These are splendid books and my pages are not intended for those already familiar with them. But Amy Carmichael is not known as she used to be, and I suspect that is because many Christians do not know the pleasure of which they are depriving themselves. In her books there are not only the tender graces that may shine in female Christian character, but also the high devotion, the fortitude, the resolution in the presence of evil, with which we all need to be inspired. It is a testimony which leads to closer fellowship with Christ, and a recognition of the better Christians we ought to be.

Many friends were involved in the production of this book. They included Ian S. Barter, Stephen Taylor, librarian of the Evangelical Library, London (an invaluable resource for authors), Ezekiel Devairakkam, Jacky Woolcock, Tahany Hanna, Margaret Holland (members of the Dohnavur Fellowship), Grace Baptist Church, Carlisle, Pa., my colleagues in the Banner of Truth Trust, and, as ever, my wife.

IAIN H. MURRAY
Edinburgh
November 2014

I

FROM BELFAST TO INDIA

Before I Was

Thou knewest me before I was,
   I am all open unto Thee,
And yet Thou lovest me, because
   My Lord, Thou lovest me.

No other reason can I find,
   No other reason can there be;
No human love, were it not blind,
   Could ever care for me.

But Thy pure eyes do read me through,
   My soul is naked unto Thee;
And yet, O wonder ever new,
   My Lord, Thou lovest me.

And Thou wilt love; if good of mine
   Had caused Thy glorious love to be,
Then surely would Thy love decline
   And weary, Lord, of me.

I may not fear, for to the end
   Thou lovest, Lord. O who but Thee,
The sinner's Saviour and his Friend,
   Would set his love on me?

And on Thee now my heart is set,
   Thy name is music unto me.
O help me never to forget
   That I am loved by Thee.

                A.C.

In India, on a street in Madras in the early twentieth century, a Britisher had a first meeting with a woman whose appearance struck him as distinctly different. It was not that she was white, for there were numbers from Britain in that part of the British Empire. But she wore a bright-coloured *sari*, and the three girls with her were clearly Indian. The short, dark-haired woman 'looked so loving and the three small children with her were so friendly and un-shy and clung to her, and were just like little blue butterflies in their blue *saris*—quite different from the usual staid children that I knew'.[1] Only later did the observer learn that this eye-catching group were visitors from Dohnavur, a village in the far south of India. The woman was Amy Carmichael, and had he first met her at Dohnavur, surrounded

[1] Frank Houghton, *Amy Carmichael of Dohnavur* (London: SPCK, 1953), p. 243. Hereafter referred to as *Houghton*.

by 200 Tamil-speaking girls, for whom she was mother, nurse and teacher, he would have been still more surprised.

To understand the story of Amy Carmichael we must go back to the beginning. Born at Millisle, Northern Ireland, on December 16, 1867, she came from the Ulster Presbyterian stock which produced generations of women whose lives moulded homes and missionary outposts across the world. Part of what they were came from their genes, another part from the heritage into which they were born. Reverence for God, the Book of Psalms, family worship and the Ten Commandments were part of the fabric of their lives. Sundays, pre-eminently, were for God and his word. It would be said of Amy, 'For the rest of her life the majestic cadences of the Authorized (King James) Version of the Bible shaped her thinking and every phrase she wrote.'

Two centuries earlier, the Carmichaels had been persecuted Scots who had seen the gospel spread in days of revival. It was a history not yet forgotten. The lessons of duty, discipline and hardship had come down through generations and, when found in Christian women of vivacious and energetic personality, the earth knew the impact. Amy Carmichael was one such Ulster woman. Born into a moderately affluent family, sent to a boarding school in England at the age of twelve, she was about fifteen when, she wrote,

> In His great mercy the Good Shepherd answered the prayers of my mother and father and many other loving ones, and drew me, even me.

At this same time the financial circumstances of her parents, David and Catherine Carmichael, underwent a reversal. Her father had prospered as a mill-owner in Millisle, and had, with his brother, William, built a new mill in Belfast. But here financial difficulties arose, severely aggravated when a large loan they had made was not repaid. This must have happened in 1883, for one year earlier her two brothers, Norman and Ernest, had been sent to King William's College, in the Isle of Man, only to be withdrawn in the summer of 1883.[2] At the same time Amy's three

---

[2] Norman (b. 1869) went to British Columbia in

years' schooling in Harrogate had to end. Life changed further for the Carmichael household (in which there were two more younger brothers and two younger sisters), when their father died suddenly on April 12, 1885, at the age of fifty-four.

At this point Amy was occupied in helping all the younger members of the family and with taking classes in painting. Then, one Sunday morning, she and her brothers met an old woman, clearly not a churchgoer, struggling to carry a heavy bundle. Ordinary as it might seem to us, the decision to stop and help marked a stage in Amy's life. An element of embarrassment was overcome as the words of Scripture came forcibly to her mind, 'Gold, silver, precious stones, wood, hay, stubble; every man's work shall be made manifest: for the day shall declare it' (1 *Cor.* 3:12-13). From this period her life would be shaped by the thought that 'Nothing is important

---

1890, and Ernest (b. 1870) to New Jersey in 1889. *King William's College Register, 1833-1927* (Glasgow: Jackson, 1928), p. 194. Their cousin, Sidney Carmichael, son of their father's colleague, had a similar short stay at the school.

but that which is eternal.' Gospel work among children in a deprived area of Belfast now became a leading interest.

She had become a Christian at a time when the truth that spiritual usefulness is related to personal holiness was gaining wider attention among evangelicals. For some it was stimulated by an annual gathering at Keswick, Cumbria, and parallel conventions were held elsewhere. At the age of eighteen Amy went to Glasgow for meetings 'on the deepening of spiritual life'. Andrew Bonar was also there and wrote in his *Diary*, 'The meetings of the Convention though sometimes a little misleading, have been helpful.'[3] In 1887, at a similar meeting in Belfast she heard Hudson Taylor and Robert Wilson.

Wilson was to play a major part in her future life. Owner of a coal mine, and a brick-making factory at Broughton in Cumbria, he was one of the founders of the Keswick Convention. After meeting the Carmichaels in Belfast, he invited Amy and her brothers to attend the Convention

---

[3] *Andrew Bonar, Diary and Life*, ed. M. Bonar (Edinburgh: Banner of Truth, 2013), p. 261.

and to stay at his home, Broughton Grange, some fifteen miles from Keswick. He had lost a daughter who had died about the age that Amy had now reached, and more recently his wife had also died, leaving him alone with two bachelor sons in the eleven-bedroom house he had built in 1859.

2. Robert Wilson, the 'Dear Old Man'.

An observer at the time of the visit of the young Carmichaels noted the 'brightness and cheerfulness' which Amy brought with her, and the same thought was not missed by Robert Wilson. Financial difficulties were now scattering the Carmichael family, and they also probably entered into the unusual request which he put to Amy's mother in 1890: could Amy be allowed to stay with them at Broughton Grange for part of each year as a kind of adopted daughter?

3. Broughton Grange, near Keswick, Cumbria.

The proposal was agreed. If it helped the Carmichaels, it certainly helped Mr Wilson. One day she happened to call him a 'Dear Old Man', and thereafter D.O.M. became the affectionate nickname. Amy recognized that he could teach her much, and she delighted in the scenery of Cumbria. Robert Wilson was a man of sixty-five years, of strong character and winsome personality. Among other things which he gave to Amy was a closer knowledge of overseas missions. This was to have a consequence which he had not intended. He prized Amy's presence at Broughton Grange, and hoped it would be her main home all his days. That prospect was not unwelcome to her, but it came to be overruled by a stronger compulsion. On July 26, 1892, she noted, 'Definitely given up for service abroad.' The next month she offered herself to the China Inland Mission (CIM), and left to be interviewed in London. She was accepted by the Mission. Her trunks were packed, and she was ready for sailing, when the Mission doctor turned her down on health grounds. Amy was joyfully received back at Broughton Grange, but not for long.

Her thoughts now turned to Japan. A letter was sent to Barclay Buxton, leader of the Japanese Evangelistic Band, and with the D.O.M.'s support, she sailed to China, en route for Japan, in March 1893.

For the next fifteen months Japan was to be a difficult but valuable training ground, where Amy threw herself into language study and evangelistic witness among the people. Some of her experiences during this time would mark the rest of her life. She learned to reject some methods of winning the attention of unbelievers which some evangelicals were adopting. She was advised, for example, 'that more girls would be drawn to meetings if she offered lessons in sewing or embroidery and administered only a mild dose of the gospel'.[4] By that means, it was said, more would listen to her speak about Jesus. But she did

---

[4] Elisabeth Elliot, *A Chance to Die, The Life and Legacy of Amy Carmichael*, (Grand Rapids: Fleming Revell, 1987), p. 84. This work is a valuable and beautifully written addition to the earlier biography by Frank Houghton. I am indebted to both volumes. Amy's letters home formed the contents of her first book, *From Sunrise Land: Letters from Japan* (London: Marshall, 1895).

not believe in such indirect dealing with people:

> I would rather have two who came in earnest than a hundred who came to play. We have no time to play with souls like this. It is not by ceremonial tea-making and flower arranging, not by wood chrysanthemum-making and foreign sewing-learning, but *by My Spirit, saith the Lord*.

Similarly, she would not follow the common practice she found among missionaries of using supposed pictures of Christ in the presentation of the gospel. This was 'unthinkable to Amy' writes Elisabeth Elliot: 'No one, she felt, had a right to presume to imagine the Son of God. Who could possibly separate manhood from Godhead? She shrank in dread from such holy ground, and reminded those who disagreed that the apostles had avoided all appeal to the senses, trusting in the power of the Word alone. The Church, she said, resorted to pictures only when her power had gone.'[5]

[5] *Chance to Die*, p. 93. In later years Amy met a child looking with disappointment at a picture of 'Jesus'. 'Oh', she said, 'I thought he was much more wonderful than that.'

A casual remark, made to her one day by another missionary, focussed her mind on a subject that would remain at the centre of her thinking. In a discussion of behaviour among missionaries it was said to her, 'You don't mean to say you think all missionaries love one another?' Amy was astonished. The words suggested to her the tolerance of failure to practise a clear command of Christ. While still in her twenties, Amy saw love as the foremost Christian grace, and as foundational to Christian living and witness.

The time in Japan seemed prematurely cut short when acute and persistent neuralgia led a doctor to question Amy's suitability for the climate. She was directed to take a rest with CIM missionaries in Shanghai. Once there, however, in July 1894, a week put Amy back on her feet, and if Japan was not the field for her, then, she believed, Ceylon (now Sri Lanka) should be. To the dismay of her hosts she departed on the first boat to Colombo. When news of this reached her patron at Broughton Grange he was concerned as well as surprised. At the age of twenty-six Amy was dependent on the Keswick Mission

Committee who funded her going out, and they knew nothing of the sudden change. Understandably, her adopted father was not happy. He wrote advising her to come home, and against her joining another mission in Ceylon. Amy's response was to write:

> Talk of coming home! Did ever a soldier, worth calling one, run away at the first shot! Praise Him—the pain is gone now, and I am strong for the battle again.

Nonetheless she did go home when she heard in November that D.O.M. had suffered a stroke. By December 15, 1894, the day before her birthday, she was back in England where her mother met her in London.

Wilson recovered, and delighted that she was 'given back', while she was glad to be at the much-loved home at Broughton. But it was not for long. She had his help and blessing in responding to an opening in the work of the Church of England Zenana Missionary Society in India. On October 11, 1895, she left Britain at the age of twenty-seven never to return.

'Zenana' was a Hindi word for the part of a house where women are kept in seclusion. After her arrival at the Mission Hospital at Bangalore, South India, Amy was to take several years to understand the full implications of that word. Meanwhile she had to learn the Tamil language, spoken by 15 million. While learning languages did not come naturally to her, it was not the language study which was most painful. She had seen something of heathenism in Japan, but here the evil, the darkness, and the demonic were more palpable. Two centuries of British rule had little touched the social structures which enslaved millions, with women and children the greatest sufferers. These structures were either endorsed or tolerated by Hinduism, the principal religion, and were left largely undisturbed by the British governing authorities for fear of upsetting the native population. Trade was the priority for too many Europeans.[6]

[6] At the same time, Amy was far from thinking that Britain had done nothing for India. 'The British Raj may have its faults', she wrote in 1914, 'but it is certainly a peacemaker.' Amy Wilson-Carmichael, *Walker of Tinnevelly* (London: Morgan and Scott, 1916), p. 275.

Hindus were born into a caste system which determined their position and trades for life. By this means the position of the poor and the weak was rendered irreversible. Women suffered most. In the majority of cases they remained servants for life and, where the practice of *suttee* continued, even in death. The *suttee* tradition required that, when a husband died, the 'true wife' showed herself by being burnt alive with him on his funeral pyre. It was not long before Amy saw this done among the Kota people; none of their number, she was told, had yet been brought to Christ.

No less a shock was it for Amy to find a formal Christianity often existing, quietly and too comfortably, in the midst of a prevailing darkness. Christian missions of various kinds had been in India for many years but, along with conversions, a large measure of formal Christianity had come into being in some areas. There were 'Christians' who neither read nor possessed Bibles, who

---

Hereafter cited as *Walker*. The inclusion of 'Wilson' in her surname, a practice followed in all her early books, indicates the closeness of the relationship with Robert Wilson.

would do Christian work only if paid to do so, and who understood the meaning of the gospel no better than the heathen. Amy wrote home, 'The saddest thing one meets is the nominal Christian ... The church here is a "field full of wheat and tares".' In Bangalore, Amy came to believe that in the face of discouragement missionaries were tempted to tone down their Christianity and to accept a degree of compromise with the prevailing conditions.

It was a very significant day for Amy when she heard Thomas Walker, a clergyman of the Church of England, working with the Church Missionary Society in the Tinnevelly district of south India. He was preaching at a convention meeting at Ooty and she had taken a Tamil grammar with her to read in case he should prove dull. She had heard reports of Walker as 'a bit narrow-minded but scholarly parson'. That image was immediately changed, yet their first meeting at Ooty gave no indication of future friendship. It was rather to his wife that Amy gravitated. But her husband's fluency in Tamil was an attraction, and when the Walkers invited her to join them in

Tinnevelly, as a better area to study the language, with a promise that he would coach her, she accepted. The Zenana work and the CMS were closely associated.

4. Thomas Walker.

By the end of 1896 Amy was with the Walkers, and so began one of the strongest influences in her life. She would later describe what her host's sermon on the first Sunday of 1897 meant to her:

The punkahs were waving sleepily on that Sunday evening, and the congregation, a few missionaries, fewer civilians, and a few Indian friends had settled down for the sermon. The preacher gave out the text: 'The powers of the world to come'. The text was read with piercing solemnity: they seemed to cut through the air like a knife. All sense of time, place and people passed suddenly; there was nothing left to think about but those great solemn powers, the powers of the world to come. A certain nervous mannerism in the speaker which would have been disturbing if the subject had not been less finely handled, was forgotten— all the personal and trivial was forgotten; this present world with its puny powers seemed as nothing, a shrivelled leaf. Only the Eternal was important. That was the sense of the hour; it deepened life for at least one who heard. But the preacher never knew.[7]

7 *Walker*, pp. 182-3.

It was part of the sense of reserve they both shared that Walker was not told by his pupil. A breakthrough in the more formal relationship came at the breakfast table one morning when Amy recounted a dream of the previous night. Clearly her daytime problem over learning Tamil came back to her in her sleep when an 'angel' asked her, 'How much do you want the language?' 'Enough to win souls, and a little over', she had replied. When her coach heard of the dream, there was a smile in his usually serious eyes as he assured her, 'You *shall* have a little over.'

Thomas Walker, born in Derbyshire in 1859, was only eight years older than Amy. He had come from Cambridge as a missionary in 1885, and married a 'Miss Hodge' of the Zenana Mission in 1890. For most of the years since his arrival he had assisted the evangelical bishops of Tinnevelly, and given much time to administrative work, but at this date he had resigned from these duties to give himself to evangelistic outreach, as well as the training of candidates for the gospel ministry. One of his journal entries indicates how teaching Tamil to Amy was an extra:

Eight a.m., prayer meeting. Tamil proof sheets (Pearson on *The Creed*). Heard of my father's death. Lord, make me hear the voice! Correspondence. Coached _____ [A.C.].[8] Evening to Savalai (a Hindu village] to Hindu Naiks.

'He was', Amy records, 'a capital teacher, very patient with stupidity, at least so his pupil at that time found him, and quick to welcome the least sign of small intelligence. For example, that particular pupil happened to be keen on the history of words; and he would hunt through his Sanskrit and Tamil dictionaries till he satisfied her on every minute question, thinking nothing a trouble if only the result was appreciated.'[9]

Amy's appreciation of her mentor deepened as she saw him as an evangelist. Walker had initiated a men's itinerating 'preaching band' which, travelling in a bullock-bandy cart with a matting cover, visited many parts of the large Tinnevelly district. While he had prayed for the help of 'two bachelors', Amy was part of the answer. Assisted

---

[8] Although Amy's presence is occasionally evident in her biography of Walker, her name nowhere appears. Square brackets in the quotation are mine.

[9] *Walker*, p. 184.

by a little group of Indian Christian women, she became the leader of a women's band as soon as she had enough of the language.

It was an experience which confirmed for her the truth of Walker's words:

> The life of an itinerating missionary is a grand school in which to learn the lesson that a man's life consisteth not in the abundance of the things which he possesseth. I can recommend it to luxurious Christians who think that they could not possibly exist without this favourite picture or that particular diet.

The busyness of the Walkers' lives was an example never to be forgotten:

> Missions were taken for Christians, and special meetings for workers, for men and women; Bible classes, meetings for prayer and prolonged waiting on God, and numberless open-air meetings for Hindus. A Sunday school for men, women and children was organized (Mrs Walker's special care), and teachers were trained.[10]

How much Amy owed to Walker it is impossible to say, but again and again in her *Walker*

[10] *Walker*, p. 187.

of Tinnevelly she highlights features which were also her own: the authors he loved;[11] the 'wordiness' and 'religious sentimentality' which he hated; the place given to prayer, to music, and poetry; the fear of 'half-conversions'; the need for separation from the world; faith in the reality of revival—all these, and more, would be mirrored in her.

One of Walker's sayings, 'Let us build for the years we shall not see', was to be fulfilled in Amy.

[11] For example, such books as the biographies those of Henry Martyn and M. Coillard, and William Arthur's *Tongue of Fire*. The habit of bringing reading to be shared at meal times was also something she learned from Walker.

5. View from the House of Prayer.

2

DOHNAVUR:
THE UNEXPECTED LIFE-CALLING

From prayer that asks that I may be
Sheltered from winds that beat on Thee,
From fearing when I should aspire,
From faltering when I should climb higher,
From silken self, O Captain, free
Thy soldier who would follow Thee.

A.C.

The house Amy came to share with the Walkers, and sometimes others, was at Pannaivilai. Originally built by missionaries, it had been occupied by rats, bats and cobwebs before Thomas Walker arrived to set it straight. It consisted of one large central room, with bedrooms on either side, and one room above, reached from a staircase from the surrounding verandah. Minimal ancient furniture, which survived from an earlier period, included the cane bed that Amy occupied in one of the downstairs rooms. At a time when there was trouble expected from intruders, Amy slept upstairs while the Walkers slept on the verandah at the foot of the stairs. Among his other gifts, the head of the house had ability in wielding a stick as he showed on at least one occasion when confronted by thieves. A compound with great mango trees and many birds, separated the building from the noise and smell of a Hindu village.

The real physical discomfort came at the time when Amy went out with the preaching bands, male and female bands usually going together, though each concentrating on witness to their own sex. Bullock carts, with solid wheels and no springs, made for the roughest travel and when night came tents were commonly their only accommodation. The caste system seldom allowed Hindus to eat with them or to sleep under their roofs. An outside veranda was usually as close as they were allowed to get and they seldom received a welcome, or were asked to come back and teach again. 'Go!' said one typical Hindu woman, 'We neither want you nor your book nor your way.' 'Who wants your Lord Jesus here?' an old leper called after them. 'Neither we nor our Gospel were desired', Amy wrote home. It brought her to consider the question posed by Isaiah, 'Shall the prey be taken from the mighty, or the lawful captive delivered?' And God's answer to that question came to mean much to her, 'But thus saith the Lord, Even the captives of the mighty shall be taken away, and the prey of the terrible shall be delivered' (Isa. 49:24-25).

Amy, with the Walkers, saw a fulfilment of that promise in 1898. Two women broke from their caste system to follow Christ and to join them. The younger had to be sent away for her safety, while the older—a twenty-three year old widow, Ponnammal—joined Amy's band and became an inseparable friend.

6. A bullock-bandy cart.

Three years later another addition had special significance. She was a seven-year-old girl,

Preena, who arrived where Amy was staying at 6.30 on the morning of March 7, 1901. In Amy's words her coming, 'caused a new thing to begin and I was rooted for life'. The girl had fled from the custody of a temple where she was being prepared, as she was told, to be 'married to the god'. It would take Amy time to learn that the words actually meant a commitment to a life of 'deified devilry'. Integral to the life of many Hindu temples was the presence of 'temple women', in reality prostitutes, trained from childhood to see their occupation as service to the gods whom they supposedly honoured. After Preena had been procured as a child, she had escaped once before and walked the twenty miles back to her home. But temple women found her, and brought her back to the punishment of having her hands branded with hot irons. On her second escape the girl had fled for refuge to a church where she was found outside, a 'very small and desolate mite with tumbled hair and troubled eyes', before being brought to Amy. Fifty years later Preena recalled that morning meeting:

Our precious Ammai was having her morning *chota*.[1] When she saw me, the first thing she did was to put me on her lap and kiss me. I thought, 'My mother used to put me on her lap and kiss me — who is the person who kisses me like my mother?' From that day she became my mother.

Later that year, four other children, not from temples, but in evident need of care, came to Amy. This presented a problem, for she was committed to itinerating with the Walkers. The remedy was to make a new base at a three-room, disused mission house at Dohnavur, where the children could be cared for while she was away. But what she had learned of temple prostitution from Preena — a state of affairs hidden from Europeans — gave her a burden for the deliverance of other temple children which would not leave her. Now she understood, as she had not before, what the temple women she met on her travels were doing when they were collecting girls. She wrote: 'We are skirting the abyss, an abyss which is deep and foul beyond description,

[1] Frank Houghton tells us that 'Ammai' means 'true mother'. *Chota* is a light early breakfast.

and yet it is glorified in Hindu eyes, by the sanctions of religion.'

* * *

Evangelical mission work in India, in the nineteenth century, often aimed to reach the sons of the upper classes, principally by the establishment of schools and colleges. The hope was that by Indians being thus educated, Christian influence would filter down to those below. It is to be questioned whether too much time was given to that policy, and whether the attention concentrated on the higher classes was consistent with the evidence to which Paul referred when he wrote: 'Ye see your calling brethren, how that not many wise men after the flesh, not many mighty, not many noble, are called: But God hath chosen the foolish things of the world to confound the wise' (*1 Cor.* 1:26-7). Amy Carmichael was called to work at the very bottom of the heap of humanity.[2]

---

[2] Not all missionaries to India, of course, followed the priority given to education. George Bowen (1816–88) of Bombay was one who did not. Roland Allen drew notable attention to the mistake of rating education too

This was a programme not simply difficult but impossible by any human effort. Prayer was foundational to what was needed. Since leaving England, supplying news to praying friends at home had been part of her life, but the necessity of intercession now had a new dimension of urgency. Yet this faced her with a problem. How could Christians at home be more urgent in prayer unless they knew of conditions as they really were? Her correspondence, sent regularly to friends, contained accounts which contrasted markedly with the bright, optimistic reports which Christians were more accustomed to receive from mission fields. So much was this the case that there was doubt at home whether what Amy wrote could be true. It was when some of her correspondents became convinced that she was describing reality, that they urged her letters should be published and read by a far larger public. But enquiries in the publishing

---

highly in his two books, *The Spontaneous Expansion of the Church* (1962), and *Missionary Methods: St Paul's or Ours?* (1962). Amy also reflected that educational work was easier than evangelism, though she valued both.

world met with no ready response. Christian publishers wanted news of success and feared that what Amy wrote would discourage missionary support, and perhaps put off candidates. One publisher returned Amy's manuscript with a request for alterations, and the advice that she should 'make it more encouraging'.

When a book made up of Amy's letters did appear in 1903 under the title *Things as They Are: Mission Work in South India*, there was critical reaction. Elisabeth Elliot reports that there was even 'a fairly strong "Get-Amy-Carmichael-out-of-India" movement'.[3] Such was the extent of the censure that, before the book was reprinted, her publisher thought it necessary to include supporting testimonies from other Christian workers in India. One of these contributors was Dr Rudisill of the Methodist Episcopal Press, Madras, who wrote: 'Miss Carmichael had given only glances and glimpses, not full insights. Let those who think the picture she has drawn too dark know that, if the whole truth were told, an evil spirit only could produce the pictures, and

[3] *Chance to Die*, p. 198.

hell itself would be the only place in which to publish them.'

Amy was not disturbed by the criticism. She had never supposed that what she wrote would be 'popular'; indeed, in later years when a Christian paper used that word to describe some of her books she was indignant: 'Popular? Lord, is that what these books written out of the heat of battle are? Popular? O Lord, burn the paper to ashes if that be true.' She was equally indignant at the idea that she wrote to 'interest' people in foreign missions. It was not 'interest' but a calling on God in blood-earnestness that she looked for. But if her account of things in South India dismayed the faint-hearted, it awoke others. In the opinion of Frank Houghton, himself later a missionary in India, 'The burden that she saw stirred thousands ... They began to pray as they have never prayed before, to take the challenge of heathenism seriously.'⁴

The letters which make up the contents of *Things as They Are* were written, in Houghton's

⁴ *Houghton*, p. 330. *Things As They Are* had gone through twelve printings by the time Houghton wrote in 1953 and remains in print today (ReadaClassic.com).

opinion, before the arrival of Preena in 1901. Only slowly did the scale and nature of the evil from which the girl had been delivered become clearer to Amy. 'It was a long time', she writes,

> before all the secret sources of traffic in the bodies and souls of children were uncovered as we penetrated deeper and deeper into the under life of the land, and came upon things that were hateful even to know.[5]

She learned of a 'dreadful underworld', and of the whole variety of means by which temple women and priests obtained girls to continue the corruption of centuries. A family vow or custom led to the dedication of children to the temple. Other girls were sold because of the destitution of their parents, or to provide the money required by the caste for the performance of death ceremonies. Once sold, a girl became the property of the temple.

For three years after Preena's rescue, no other baby or temple child could be found and brought into care. Then, on March 1, 1904, an unwanted

[5] Amy Carmichael, *Gold Cord, The Story of a Fellowship*, (1932; reprint ed., Fort Washington, Pa.: CLC, 1999), p. 50.

baby, born of a temple woman, and just thirteen days old, was put into Amy's hands. Through various circumstances two other babies followed. Then a girl, Lavana, who had become a Christian, defied her parents' call for her to return home. When the parents promised her jewels, she replied, 'I don't want jewels, I have Jesus now.'

When some in England questioned whether this was not endorsing disobedience to parents, Amy enlightened them with evidence of what could happen to converts who broke caste. They could be induced to return home only to be instantly married, or treated to mind-bewildering drugs, or thrown down wells, or simply to disappear never to be heard of again. Breaking caste was a 'sin' grave enough to justify retribution of all kinds. On one occasion Amy had a frail baby in her care in desperate need of a mother's milk. With difficulty, she obtained the consent of a village woman to save its life by breast-feeding. But in so doing the woman broke caste, and for this her husband killed her by slow arsenic poisoning. Fear of breaking caste tyrannised society. Amy met a mother who preferred to see her suffering infant die rather than to break caste by allowing Amy to give the child hospital care.

The presence of the three additional babies in 1904 was only short-lived. The temples wanted healthy, attractive girls, and perhaps it was because the physical condition of these babies offered no such prospect that their parents did not want them. Despite every effort for them, all three little ones died, the last on January 6, 1905. Amy responded by making the sixth day of every month a day of prayer for children in danger.

By June 1904, seventeen children, six of them former temple children, were in Amy's care, and even when the number was depleted by the death of the three babies, it was clear that her evangelistic travels had to end. 'Children tie the feet' was a Tamil saying. She would not have let her feet be so tied had she not been convinced that God meant her to be the full-time 'mother' of 'the family' now being gathered. Her life-work had been given to her.

By this time the Walkers and Amy were no longer living at Pannaivilai. In 1900 Thomas Walker had decided that a disused Church

Missionary Society mission station at a place thirty miles north of Cape Comorin—India's southern point—would be a better and quieter site for the ordination classes he took for divinity students. This was Dohnavur, a 'Christian' village which he had first visited in 1886. The name came from a German supporter of missions, Count Dohna, and *ur* meaning village. In 1824, a white-washed church had been built by money provided by Dohna. Close to the church was a compound, with a 'bare barn-like bungalow', and a few huts, which Walker came to prepare for accommodation in June 1900. For some the site, on a plain of red earth without vegetation save for trees, may have had little appeal, but when Amy and the women's band arrived on June 21, 1900, she loved it from the start: 'The whole place was charming.' Less than a mile to the west was a shallow lake and, immediately beyond, the jungle-clad mountains of the Southern Ghauts rising steeply above the plain:

> The south-west monsoon had cooled the air and covered the mountains with veils of light mist, so that they looked like the mountains of

home, only higher and grander; for in India, even in the south, the hills run from five thousand to over eight thousand feet … all this was pure delight, and from the first happy day of arrival it was a place of song.[6]

In 1900, however, Amy did not see the location in terms of a permanent home but rather as a base, in an 'exceedingly needy' and 'very strongly Hindu' area. It would appear that the life of Dohnavur village had done little to affect the adjacent Pulliankurichi ('village of the tiger'), or to touch the nearly 3,000 Hindu temples in the Tinnevelly area. She wrote in 1932, 'There were thousands of temple women in this single Presidency. It was (and is) an overwhelming thought.'[7] Not lightly were the words, 'He must reign', hung up in the bungalow which would become the 'best-loved Indian home'.

The commitment to the children, which Amy came to by 1904, was not an alternative to her passion for all age groups to be brought to Christ. It was very much a part of it. Yet the itinerating

[6] *Walker*, p. 273.
[7] *Gold Cord*, p. 42.

side had now to be left more largely to Walker. He came to share her vision for the children, and events could hardly have unfolded as they did without his support. When she adopted Indian dress, 'he—almost alone in the missionary community—approved and stood behind her'.[8] The truth was that, with her dark hair and brown eyes, her nationality might have been mistaken. It probably was at times, when she stained her hands and arms with coffee to look for temple children in places where foreign women would never have been admitted. All eyes were brown in India, except those of foreigners. Blue eyes would have made her occasional disguise useless. This little detail was a reminder to her of a childhood incident. She had far preferred her mother's blue eyes to her own, and acting on the instruction that 'Jesus always answers prayer', she had asked for blue eyes like her mother's. Disappointment followed, and she was struggling to understand how a promise could not be true when Catherine Carmichael assured her that it was true: 'He does answer but an answer may be "No".' Only in

[8] *Houghton*, p. 97.

later years was she learning that a 'No' may be better than 'Yes'.

Walker's part in the developing endeavour made new demands on his time. One night in March 1903, his journal records, he left Dohnavur at midnight, when he heard that a girl had been 'carried off forcibly' by relatives after a court had determined she should be put in Christian care. Walker went straight to the magistrate and chief of police, but the girl had been hidden, and by the time she appeared again in court she had been drugged and 'married'. At which point she was handed back to her people. In subsequent years Walker would repeatedly be involved in court appearances for children in danger. While appeals in the British courts were not always successful, they certainly offered far more justice than could be obtained from any Hindu priests. So Amy found on one occasion when she went alone to speak to a priest who had been head of the Benares temple. She had heard that he might be a person who would listen to an appeal. It was not to be:

We found ourselves in the presence of one of the men who control this secret traffic. Half animal, half demon, he sat, a coiled mass of naked flesh. The window-shutters of that upper room were closed, though the night was hot; the room was full of sickly fumes; a yellow flame flickered in a corner. It was an evil room. We could not speak, but turned defeated, and, climbing down the steep and slimy stairs, escaped into the cleaner air of the street.

The hope of any deliverance from that direction had only been froth.

The strength of Walker's leadership in the early days at Dohnavur was vital but, before 1904 ended, Amy had to take on that role herself. Mrs Walker had been seriously ill and when her husband took her to a doctor in Madras he received the direction that she must be taken out of the tropics at once. So, with the prayer, 'Lord, undertake, arrange, shield', the Walkers left for England in December 1904. 'I stood', wrote Amy, 'on the verandah of our three-roomed bungalow, listening to the scrunch of the wheels of the bullock-cart as it turned on the rough gravel and drove unwillingly away.'

The only regular helpers Amy now had for the care of her charges were two Indian Christian women. It was far less than what was needed. There were now dormitories, nurseries, kitchens, a weaving shed and gardens, all to be looked after. With watchfulness needed at night as well as in the day, Amy believed they could not have survived without the help of angels. She knew of occasions when it was their presence which prevented a fatality. After a long day's work, and asleep in her room, she was prompted awake by a feeling that something was wrong in a nursery. On going there, and listening quietly outside, she found all peaceful and decided the premonition was mistaken. But somehow, as she turned to go back to her bed, she was pulled up by a sense that she must go inside. On doing so she found that Balana, one of the dozen babies, had become so tied up in the tapes holding her in her hammock that she was strangling and unable to cry out. 'I was just in time to cut the tapes.' Years later, when these infants were grown up, she would write of the 'unseen guardians of their childhood' and think that they would 'feel repaid for their vigils by those little white hammocks, and for many a walk across to our rooms at night to call us to come'.

If, as Jesus says of little ones, 'that in heaven their angels do always behold the face of my Father'(*Matt.* 18:10), it was no problem for Amy to believe that angels have a ministry of preservation on earth.[9] In that connexion, with reference to Walker's absence, she would write, 'The angel guard was doubled round Dohnavur through the months when it was left without its human guard.'

Amy was learning something greater than this. When loneliness or sorrow threatened to overtake her, she believed it 'was His burden not mine. It was He who was asking me to share it with Him, not I who was asking Him to share it with me.' It was, she felt, as though the tamarind trees around the house were the olives under which Jesus knelt. The 'holy Son of God' was present. Yet tears could attend his work. 'God's choicest wreaths are always wet with tears.'[10]

[9] *Gold Cord*, p. 87.
[10] *Overweights of Joy* (London: Morgan and Scott, 1906), p. 131.

7. Amy with the girls at the beach.

3

AMY'S GIRLS

O dear Lord Jesus,
    Thou lovest me,
I do not know at all
    How that can be.

But, dear Lord Jesus,
    I know it's true,
True as that grass is green,
    And skies are blue.
So, dear Lord Jesus,
    Help me to be
Thy loving little child,
    Pleasing to Thee.[1]

A.C.

---

[1] *Dohnavur Songs* (2002), p. 48.

Thomas Walker began a return voyage to India at the end of October 1905, but his wife's health was such that she had to remain in England for a further year. For a time her absence would be made up by the arrival of another helper in the person of Amy's mother, whom Walker was to treat with 'the devotion of a son'.

When Catherine Carmichael arrived at Dohnavur, late in 1904, she found a family of over thirty, 'ranging in age from thirty-four years to a babe of nine months', and wrote home: 'Since we came here a month ago I can truthfully say [Amy] has scarcely had leisure even to eat. She is mother, doctor, and nurse, day and night.'

Much had happened in the near derelict compound since 1900. The property was renovated, new buildings erected, and gardens established. To all the children Amy was 'Amma' (mother). She was described, not as walking but as 'flying' to attend to the many needs. The children came to nick-name her 'the Hare'. In time she would use a tricycle to move even faster between the various buildings.

Catherine Carmichael, after fifteen busy months, had to return to England in 1906. That same year there was evident answer to prayer for a spiritual change among the young people, 'a work began among us which was like the fall of dew on grass', and Amy had joy beyond her ability to express, as six confessed Christ and were baptized early in 1907. This was followed, as so often happened, by new difficulties. Dysentery had become prevalent in the area and, in the serious illness brought into Dohnavur, Amy was laid aside. She was 'ordered home' but instead took to the hills which she loved.[1]

In her absence the Walkers carried on, but it seems Mrs Walker's health never fully recovered, and he had many other duties besides contributing to what Amy had begun. Amy would later record that initially the Walkers 'had been troubled about the very firm tying of our feet; but upon Mr Walker's return he had written to Indian

[1] *Gold Cord*, p. 73.

converts who knew the underworld of India, and after he read the ghastly letters that came in reply, he ceased to doubt. It was more than worthwhile to turn from all else, he felt, and save the children.' 'He was always', she writes further, 'on the lookout for anything which would give the children pleasure; and naturally the children were devoted to him.' An Indian worker recalled how he went round the compound every evening, checking on everyone's welfare: 'He used to let us bring a stool out of the nursery, and then he would sit among the children telling them stories for half an hour.'

As time went on and the 'tinies' grew up there was the additional need of schooling. It became another role for Amy and one in which she soon came to need help. Walker appealed to Christian friends at home:

> I am writing now to ask you to be on the look out, during your travels, for a lady suited to take educational charge of _____ [Amy's] children. God may lead you to the very one. You know our position as to God's Word, and thorough evangelical principles, as also that spirituality is of the first importance. If a lady

goes to an ordinary college or high school in India, she has to fall in with the Government curriculum and with established methods of work. Here she would find, I trust, a warm spiritual atmosphere, and an unusually happy family life, and would be able to train Tamil teachers in her own way. ... I consider it a unique sphere for one who loves children and is a real educationalist. And there are great possibilities of the children becoming a unique missionary force.[2]

The first white person to come from Britain to settle at Dohnavur was Mabel Wade. She arrived unexpectedly on November 15, 1907, after 18 hours' travelling in a bullock cart, and it is an illustration of the pressure of life at Dohnavur that Amy and her two helpers were so tied up with duties that they could scarcely pause to welcome her. A trained nurse from Yorkshire, Mabel simply joined in the work at once, the first in a line of dedicated women and men who served to make 'the family' what it became. Mabel would have been an admirable help in Amy's growing school, but learning Tamil, and then attending

[2] *Walker*, p. 446.

to nursing, had to come first, and it seems it was only 'in singing and a delightful musical drill' that her aid could be given. Mrs Walker took the care of 'middle-aged babies', but lack of help meant that a kindergarten for the present had to close.

Given the need, it would have been understandable to accept the help of all who volunteered. Instead Amy was strongly committed to the qualifications given in Walker's letter above, and two would-be teachers, who came with the recommendation of Christians, were turned down.

> In each case truth was the rock on which they foundered. If our children were to grow up truthful they must be taught by those who had a regard for truth; and not just a casual regard. On this point we were adamant.

The work at Dohnavur found it difficult to hear of possible teachers from pastors and churches in India. Probably one reason for this lack was the view in some circles that Amy was too 'fastidious', if not 'narrow minded', in her choice of helpers. More commonly, however, an explanation can be traced to the fact that evangelicals were unaccustomed to think in terms of the education of lower-class girls; such a programme hardly existed in India, and few saw any urgency for its provision.

Amy took the need very seriously and had a definite understanding of what she wanted. First, the objective of schooling must be the formation of character, not merely a training of the intellect. That meant that love was the starting point, to be taught in the first instance by example. Not a child went to sleep at night without a kiss from Amy, and even when the numbers ultimately made that impossible, as long as she could, she sought to see each child every day. Commonly the birth date of the children was unknown, so, as a substitute, the 'Coming date' of each girl to Dohnavur was celebrated, and their bedroom decked with flowers. As much as possible everything characteristic of an institution was avoided. As already mentioned, the family was made up of separate nurseries, with a small group of children in the care of a 'mother'.

Education was not in order to bring a rise in social standing, or material prosperity. It was preparation to serve Christ and others. Learning Scripture was therefore foundational, and at Dohnavur this was made as appealing as possible. Just as Amy wanted her girls dressed in bright colours (especially blue!), she wanted them to see Christianity as the source of a truly happy life. Music, song and hymns served that purpose. She was herself a musician, and an artist with words as well as pictures. Many truths and observations from nature were put into verse by her to be sung by the children. Yet care was taken that song should not be an end in itself. She believed Walker's words, written after recent experience of Conventions in England:

> Let us use hymns more than ever but let us live them out! Let us sing of holiness by all means, but may He give us the grace of practical godliness in daily life. Let us sing with our Master who still leads the praises of His church, but let us be willing to suffer with Him too. Real hymn-singing leads to the singer's becoming God's 'corn of wheat', which falls into the ground and dies, and so brings forth much fruit.[3]

[3] From a South Indian Prayer Circular, *Walker*, p. 451.

Teaching was to be made as appealing as possible. This was not the same as being as entertaining as possible. The years of childhood were too important to be filled with temporary amusement. She wanted them to take in what they would need for life, and agreed whole-heartedly with the words of Arnold of Rugby on the importance of memorization,

> It is a great mistake to think they should *understand* all they learn; for God has ordered that in youth the memory should act vigorously, independent of the understanding.

Whole sections of Scripture were therefore repeated aloud — 1 Corinthians 13 every Monday morning — and whole chapters were learned by some. One child was even encouraged to proceed to the study of the Greek New Testament.

Along with the Bible, the book of creation was a constant study. Animals, flowers, trees, birds and much more, were all to be enjoyed and to be the subject of study. The children had their own gardens, and sometimes their own pets; they learned how to see chlorophyll in the leaves of plants and to study drops of water through a microscope. There were outings to 'the forest' in the mountains where there was swimming and fun as well as learning. Amy was known to startle them by her fine imitations of the growls of bears and tigers. At other times the outing was to Joppa, a favourite place on the coast near Cape Comorin. Walker could write of Amy's children:

> They know far more than I was ever taught — even the tinies — about flowers, insects, birds *etc.*, and are very much alive on the observation side of things.

In all this the love was not sentimental. There were punishments as well as encouragements. Childhood larks met with no severity, but untruthfulness did. While the children could sell items from their own vegetable garden, they received no prizes for work done. 'The great reward', they were told, 'was to be trusted with harder, more responsible work.'[4]

A number of the sayings she would use or invent would long be remembered: 'Faithfulness in little things is a very great thing'; 'Never about to, always to do'; 'Joy is not gush. Joy is

---

[4] For further information see *Chance to Die*, p. 254.

not jolliness. Joy is perfect acquiescence in God's will.' 'Let nothing be said about anyone unless it passes through the three sieves: Is it true? kind? necessary?'

Her conviction that the foundations of character must be laid in truth led her to some views on the content of education which could be a surprise to new helpers. Amy reports:

> One day a guest who afterwards became a beloved fellow-worker, gathered the children together and told them a fairy story, and then we discovered (I had hardly realized it before) that I had instinctively left those tales, and had begun with the far more magical true fairy stories that were strewn everywhere just waiting to be told.
>
> And we saw no reason to change. It was good when the amazed children asked, *Me than a* (Is it true indeed?), to be able to answer *Me than* (True indeed), and those true fairy tales were so wonderful and so beautiful that I do not think our little lovable lost anything of the silvery glamour that should make the first years of childhood like moonlit water to look back on.[5]

[5] *Gold Cord*, p. 83.

We may suppose that Mrs Walker's participation was limited by her health, and her husband's certainly by his own duties. Divinity students were under his care, and he was frequently called to take missions in various parts of India. But in the endeavour to rescue children from a life as temple women, which was on-going, he played a vital part, especially when it came to speaking on their behalf in court cases. There were numbers of these in 1910 and 1911. In Amy's words, 'the storm broke upon us and we were plunged into a welter of troubles'. A crucial case concerned Muttamal, or 'Jewel', as Amy named her. The circumstances were unusual. The girl's high-caste father was deceased, and an evil-living mother had brought her as a twelve year-old to Dohnavur in March 1909. Although this was legally confirmed by a court document, relatives, with an eye to wealth left by Jewel's father, came to appeal it on the grounds that the child's caste was being broken. At the High Court in Madras, Sir Charles Spencer dismissed the appeal, but Muttamal's uncle persisted. He waited for another court, a different judge (with no sympathy for evangelicals) and had the case re-opened. Amy had to appear in court,[6] but it was Walker, through three months in 1911, who had repeatedly to be in Madras for extended court hearings. 'Arguments not all heard', he wrote in his journal on February 28, 1911, 'and so postponed. God deliver her!' The final decision came on March 27, when he noted: 'Written judgment in little M's case against us *in toto*. A bad time altogether. Application for stay of execution treated with scant courtesy. Got off to Dohnavur alone at 10 p.m.'

On these brief entries in Walker's journal, Amy would later comment that a reader could not imagine what this battle had meant to him. Yet the re-possession of M. was not to be. When Walker arrived home at daybreak the next day it was to find that the girl had disappeared. The night before, Amy had encouraged Mabel Beath,

---

[6] When this less-than-sympathetic judge said at one point in a hearing, 'I hope you understand Miss Carmichael, that I am giving you most exceptional treatment?', he cannot have been expecting the nature of her reply, 'Yes, I quite understand that you are giving us *most* exceptional treatment.'

a British woman who was visiting Dohnavur, to take her away, disguised as a Muslim boy. Police searches were immediate and extensive, an Indian would later even visit the Beath home in London in an attempt to find the girl. The truth was she had been passed on to Christians in Ceylon, and, finally, to missionaries in China. Amy, who risked imprisonment and had to pay all the court costs,[7] had to wait six months to hear of Jewel's whereabouts. It would be six years before, happily married, she returned to the home in which she delighted at Dohnavur.

During the same critical months of court appearances in Madras, Thomas Walker was seeing the increasing ill-health of his wife and having to make preparations for another return to England. They sailed in April 1911 and he had to return alone in October, with the hope that his wife would soon be able to follow. By this date he was both an elder brother and a father to Amy and one can imagine his conversations with her of conditions in England where he had come to

---

[7] The amount was met by a payment from her publisher which arrived at the same time.

'feel a stranger in spite of relations and friends'. He thought there were reasons to be concerned about the state of things there. His experience, he told her, had been a medley of

> the inspiring and the disappointing; on the whole the note of disappointment predomi-nated. He did not always find, even among true Christians, the depth for which he looked; there was less intensity of purpose, and a greater worldliness than he expected, and a startling increase in pleasure-loving and luxurious living. He rejoiced when he met earnestness, and old-fashioned spirituality and unworldliness. ... The absence, too, of the definite surprised him; it was as if the old land-marks of principle were being swept away, and in their place he seemed to see mere borders of pretty flowers: 'So and so has a hard time of it because of his Protestantism, and yet he is working among avowed Evangelicals', he said, speaking of a well-known Church worker; 'it's as if people were so afraid of intolerance that they are beginning to have no convictions at all. ... There is something wrong in the Home churches that this missionary famine is upon us, and that at a time when doors are opening

so widely.'[8]

He felt the pain of his wife's absence, but plunged back into all his work. A new room had been built for the lectures to his students, and he delighted to show it to the children. He did not resume his Sunday Bible readings to the workers, for he was often absent from home on Sundays, taking missions and helping other missionaries. On Sunday, August 11, Amy recalled, he came to breakfast with a smile and asked, 'Do you know where we are in the Psalms?' He had evidently been revising and quoted the words which preceded the doxology at the end of Psalm 41, 'Thou upholdest me ... and settest me before thy face for ever.' 'Isn't that a good place to leave off?'

After tea that Sunday afternoon, he played with the children according to custom, giving

[8] *Walker*, pp. 434-5. A little later he wrote to his wife, 'It makes one anxious about Britain's future, for an Empire on which true religion seems to be losing its hold is in a precarious condition.' His sense of the direction Britain was taking is echoed in the life of his contemporary Archibald Brown (see Iain H. Murray, *Archibald G. Brown: Spurgeon's Successor*, [Edinburgh: Banner of Truth, 2011]).

two specially beloved little five-year-old girls rides on his foot, and rides round the room on his shoulder. Amy's biography of her friend continued:

> Next morning, as usual he read the Psalms for the day at morning tea out in the compound. It was some little time before dawn, and the moon, almost full, gave light enough for the meal; as the sun rose the two lights met, and in that mysterious blend of silver and gold light he read the beautiful Psalm. 'Thus have I looked for thee in holiness, that I might behold thy power and glory', was the last verse talked over.

That morning, he filled his bandy so full he could hardly get in: 'Then came a quick Good-bye. It was the kind of Good-bye he would have chosen; no sentiment about it: "God be with you", and he was off, deep in his *Expositor*[9] before he reached the gate. At the gate stood Sundarie, faithful servant and friend over whose baptism he had rejoiced fourteen years ago,

[9] A monthly theological journal, founded by the publishers, Hodder and Stoughton in 1875, and edited by W. Robertson Nicoll from 1885 to his death in 1923.

"*Salaam, Sundarie!* I go and come", he called out to her in the idiom of the country. "*Salaam, Iya!* Go and come", she returned.'[10]

That same week, Lulla, one of the children of the previous Sunday afternoon's gathering, was suddenly affected by one of the illnesses which could come with such speed in the East. Early on the following Sunday morning she was in such pain, 'struggling for breath and looking to us for something we could not give', that Amy left her bedside to go and pray that she would be taken quickly:

> I was not more than a minute away, but when I returned she was radiant. Her little lovely face was lighted up with amazement and happiness. She was looking up and clapping her hands as delighted children do. When she saw me she stretched out her arms, and flung them round my neck, as though saying good-bye, in a hurry to be gone; then she turned to the others in the same eager way, and then again, holding out her arms to Someone whom we could not see, she clapped her hands. Had only one of us seen this thing, we might have

---

[10] *Walker*, p. 453.

doubted. But we all three saw it. There was no trace of pain in her face. She was never to taste of pain again. We looked where she was looking, almost thinking that we would see what she saw. What must the fountain of joy be if the spray from the edge of the pool can be like that?[11]

This was comfort Amy needed for there were to be more bereavements on the road ahead. First came news of Mrs Hopwood's death, a woman who, ever since 1898, had been 'like a mother' to Amy and whose home up the mountains had ever been a second home to her. Then came the greater shock. Walker's hostess where he was staying died of cholera; then, after hours of delirium, on the morning of August 24, 1912, he also was with Christ. Near the end, thinking he was teaching his class, he said, 'You know we have come to the last chapter.' Then, although in the extremity of weakness, 'he sat up in bed, and, thinking himself alone, said aloud, "I am so happy."'

The Saviour sends comfort to those who grieve through human hands. Mrs Walker had known

[11] *Gold Cord*, p. 146.

that comfort by the time she wrote to Amy to console her. Others, nearer at hand, rallied. One of them was Mr Carr, from Palamcottah, who played the organ every evening while the children sang. Amy believed that for Christians death was never to be lamented. It had been a custom at Dohnavur to sing every Sunday night as the closing hymn, 'For all the saints'. Of that hymn, Amy was to say, 'all through the days, and often through the night, that song sings with me,

> And when the strife is fierce,
>   the warfare long,
> Steals on the ear
>   the distant triumph song,
> And hearts are brave again
>   and arms are strong,
>   Alleluia! Alleluia!'

8. Amma with her beloved children.

4

HARD DAYS AND GOLDEN YEARS

9. '"Do you really think you are like us, do we eat the same kind of curry?" This is a very respectable woman; but look at the face till you understand it, and then try to think how many ideas you and she would have in common.' A.C. *Things As They Are*, p. 262.

If there was any pattern to Amy Carmichael's life it was of times of refreshing then of trials, of exhilarating 'climbing' then of walking in dark ravines. In part her explanation was that demonic activity follows the work of the Holy Spirit. As she quoted from George Bowen,

> When Christianity assumes an aggressive attitude the first result is a great exhibition of Satanic power. Satan's power to be manifested must be assaulted.[1]

Such an understanding does not come so readily to us who do not live, as she did, within sight of demon possession, or within hearing of tom-tom drums calling devotees to idols.

Shortly before Walker had left on his last mission, he had been sitting with Amy and others in deck chairs under the stars. 'We had been talking', she later wrote,

[1] *Overweights of Joy*, p. 45.

of work and workers, and of those (to me) most wonderful women, who seemed perfectly self-reliant, needing no strong arm alongside. I remember how, suddenly startled at the bare thought of working alone, in the sense of all the burden of responsibility, I exclaimed that I never could do it. Mr Walker laughed. 'Well, you don't have to', he said.[2]

Amy was the weaker when her 'strong arm' died at the age of fifty-four. What she owed to Walker's 'courageous championship' of the children's work, 'through its first very difficult years, no words can tell, nor can words tell how he is missed'.[3] At times, as she faced her loss, she would need to say to herself, 'Don't give up, don't be afraid: go on.' Prayer for 'fortitude' entered her life.

There were unsympathetic neighbours who observed the work at Dohnavur who supposed that Amy would now be more vulnerable. One of these was a lawyer who, soon after Walker's death, wrote with the demand that current work on the building of a wall around the compound

[2] *Houghton*, p. 174
[3] *Walker*, p. ix.

be stopped, and that a half-built nursery should be pulled down. They were using ground, he claimed, to which they did not have legal title. 'He had waited till Mr Walker's death had left us, as he thought, defenceless, almost desolate, and sure to be easily cowed by threats of court trouble.'

The wall building had been prompted by the passage of a tiger through the compound at night; and the new nursery was necessitated by the growing numbers of children for whom Dohnavur had become home. Amy ignored the letter and heard nothing more of the threat.

The Dohnavur family of seventy children and grown-ups in 1906, had doubled itself by this date, and the need of more helpers was pressing. Mrs Catherine Carmichael was never able to return. She died on July 14, 1913. A few weeks earlier a letter from her to Amy began with the words, 'My own most precious earthly possession'. While Amy did not lament her mother's death—for no Christian death was to be 'lamented'—in the days ahead she needed to preach to herself, 'I must remind myself to live in the joy of those gone, not grovel in the sense of my loss.'

Mrs Carmichael had been a constant supporter and representative for Dohnavur in Britain. She acted as the home secretary to whom gifts could be sent, and helped to make her daughter's books more widely known. In 1912 those books had been noted by Queen Mary, wife of King George V, who expressed her thanks for them.

While Amy was busy in 1913 writing *Walker of Tinnevelly*, there came the possibility of the loss of her closest female friend and helper, Ponnammal, who had been with her ever since, as a young widow, she had come to new life through Walker's preaching. She now needed surgery for cancer and Amy went with her to a Salvation Army Hospital at Neyyoor for a period. In their absence from Dohnavur (forty-six miles away), and the absence of Mabel Wade who was on furlough, 70 of the children were ill. The need for more medical facilities at Dohnavur itself was evident. After much suffering, through which she was enabled to pass triumphantly, Ponnammal died in 1915, leaving her daughter to Amy's care.

These same years were matched with much encouragement. New staff arrived who would be mainstays in years ahead. Walker's former assistant and a convert of earlier years, Arul Dasan, became Amy's helper; he was able to undertake many things, from the growing of vegetables to the taking of services. Women of Amy's spirit who came to settle in the Dohnavur family included Frances Beath, Agnes and Edith Naish, and Frances Nosworthy. Of special joy to Amy was the way 'the wind blew through us as a family' in 1912. The occasion was the preaching visit of a visitor, R. T. Archibald, a man specially used of God in speaking to children. 'There was', writes Amy,

> a true conviction of sin, true repentance, honest confession and a change of life that lasted. Not one child then converted went back. Some are mothers of families now, and some are our fellow workers here.[4]

Thirty were baptized in 1913.

A change in the financial support of the work was observable at this time. After several years when unsolicited gifts had been enough to cover expenses, there had come a surplus which could

[4] *Gold Cord*, p. 156.

be laid aside. The outbreak of world war in August 1914 was to show the significance of this surplus. The British pound dwindled in value until, at one point, it fell to four shillings—less than a quarter of its pre-war value. The exchange rate soared, and so did prices. Now it cost fifteen times more to bring a child to Dohnavur from the nearest station. Rice, the most needed daily commodity, was similarly affected. Additional ground, which Amy had purchased not long before, became the more valuable as it produced food supplies under Arul Dasan's care. 'We have never lacked one good thing', Amy could write; 'and during the years of the war, people of the towns and villages began to say, "God is there"; for they could not account for what they saw except by saying that.'[5]

Amy could never settle down to an acceptance of the fact that there were so many thousands of Hindus and Muslims, accessible from Dohnavur yet living without any hope in Christ. She dreaded a dull acquiescence to the situation, and believed that a hindrance to God's working might

[5] *Gold Cord*, p. 140.

'be found in us':

> There may be weakness, compromise, lack of
> determination to keep the winning of souls
> to the front, the use of unconsecrated means,
> unsanctified ways of getting money, uncon-
> verted workers. There may be an absence of
> identification with the people for whose sake
> we are here, an unconscious aloofness not
> apostolic. Perhaps our love has cooled. Per-
> haps we know little of the power of the Holy
> Ghost, and hardly expect to see souls saved
> here and now, and are not broken down before
> the Lord because we see so few. God forgive
> us and make us more in earnest.[6]

Others at Dohnavur were to carry on the
itinerant evangelism that Amy had followed in
earlier years. But at times she herself continued
to make visits to dark corners. No one was with
her, save a young convert girl, when she faced
Brahman leaders near their temple quarters. They
laughed at her and declared, 'You are alone, and
you see how many we are. This is how the case
stands all over India.' There were other occasions
when, with an element of disguise, she entered

---

[6] *Overweights of Joy*, p. 132.

buildings shut to foreigners looking for children, or stood 'by night in the doorway of the temple, with the sculptured pillars about us, monstrous in the gloom, and the lights glittering around the idol shrine where no alien foot may tread'.[7] From such scenes she could withdraw with a sense of defeat and 'a haunting sense of impotence'.[8] Her efforts seemed like 'a snow flake falling on the Great Pyramid, melting and vanishing as it touched the hot stone'. Then she would preach to herself,

> Not to yield is all that matters. Failure or success as the world understands these words, is of no eternal account. To be able to stand steady in defeat is in itself a victory.[9]

But conversions continued. Not normally of a number at the same time, as happened in 1912, yet that occasion was not unique. One day a man

---

[7] *Gold Cord*, p. 293.

[8] I quote here from *Gold Cord*, p. 293, where she also comments, 'It is a deadly mistake to underestimate Hinduism.'

[9] *Gold by Moonlight* (1935; reprint ed., London: SPCK, 1960), p. 169. She was passing on to others what she had first said to herself.

was mauled by a tiger and brought to Dohnavur for help. He was treated, recovered, converted and went back to his village to witness. This brought a call for preachers to go to them, and when two of the men from Dohnavur went they found a courtyard of people waiting who 'would have listened all night'. Conversions, persecution and baptisms followed, and a little church was established which would stand firm.[10] Persecution was not to be dreaded, in Amy's words, 'It winnows the grain; we do not want a church of chaff.'

It is true that professed conversions did not always stand, and this was one of the greatest sorrows to be faced. But Amy would give no place to cynicism.

> Better to be disappointed a thousand times—yes, and be deceived—than once miss a chance to help a soul. The love of God suffices for any disappointment, for any defeat. And in that love is the energy of faith and the very sap of hope.

* * *

[10] *Gold Cord*, p. 334.

10. The Forest House.

Through the years of the First World War, and on into the 1920s, the work at Dohnavur grew, more land was bought, and by 1923 there were thirty nurseries, each with a mother for the children. For escape from the heat in the hottest months, a Forest house was built up in the mountains, and another retreat was obtained at Joppa on the sea coast. These became prized holiday places for the children as well as refreshing places for Amy and her helpers. As well as workers from

India, Britain and Ireland, others would come from Australia, New Zealand and Canada.

By 1923, Amy, who had been long accustomed to 'think in terms of bullock carts, not motors', acceded to the need to change the bullock-bandy for a Ford car. It was a valuable addition.[11]

Commonly Amy was given hope of what God might do before she saw any fulfilment. One such hope grew out of her concern for boys. Not at first did she recognize that male infants were also acquired by the temple priests for evil purposes. They were wanted, for instance, to be acolytes attending the gods in processions,[12] to act in immoral plays, or to become the property of homosexuals. From 1912 she made this a matter of prayer. Although she asked God to take her burden about it away, or show her what to do, she had to wait. Then late one evening in

[11] She has a chapter on 'The Ford Car' in *Tables in the Wilderness* (Madras: SPCK, 1923), a small book on how financial needs were being met.

[12] This may sound harmless enough until it is remembered, as Elisabeth Elliot writes: Amy 'believed that the gods of India, as described by their aggressive or seductive images, were satanic, and they that made them were "like unto them".' *Chance to Die*, p. 243.

January 1918 an event made action unavoidable. A needy child was handed in, and was put in a nursery before it was discovered that it was a boy. By 1926 there was to be a boys' compound with some seventy to eighty children.

Another hope, and seemingly the more difficult for fulfilment, concerned the need for a hospital and doctors at Dohnavur. As already noted, when there was serious illness the help needed was not at hand. There were cases such as Lulla's, in 1912, when assistance had to be called from elsewhere only to arrive too late. Amy has written of how her hope became a very definite prayer for eight of them one evening, January 30, 1921, as they stood together in the sunset, looking over the plain. 'We could see clusters of trees', she recalled,

> each telling of a village; to east and south and north we saw temple towers; behind one little conical hill lay a small fortress of Islam, a place of many frustrations. And we wondered why there was no medical mission in this part of British India specially bent on reaching those who are practically unaffected by the gospel.

This vision was not for medicine as an alternative to evangelism, but for doctors who would simultaneously be witnesses to the needy. Three years later Dohnavur came to have three medical doctors. They were May Powell, and the Neill family, in which both parents were physicians. In this family there were also a daughter and a son, Stephen, who had just left Cambridge where he was a fellow of Trinity College. There had hardly been such a distinguished addition to the work as the Neill family. Amy may have had doubts how easily a group of this weight and influence as the Neills would fit into work which she had led since Walker's death. As it was, the medical work went forward, first in sheds, then later, in a complete hospital, opened as 'the Place of Heavenly Healing'. This, however, was without the presence of any of the Neills. The Neill parents had some difference with Amy over where a new hospital should be built, whether as part of the Dohnavur compound or elsewhere. They had only stayed six months. But Stephen Neill remained and it was with him that the more serious disagreement occurred. Although not yet ordained in the ministry of the Church of England, his parents believed that, with a Cambridge education behind him, and having learned Tamil in an astonishing six months, Stephen was better qualified than Amy to lead and supervise Christian instruction.

But Dohnavur was not Cambridge, and the difference was not merely in the appearance of things. The whole approach to the Bible in Britain's university world had undergone a major change. Some, including Neill, thought that a change of belief over the trustworthiness of Scripture could be accommodated within 'a new type of Evangelicalism'.[13] His subsequent history shows that this was his view, and there can be little doubt that it was already being formed when he came to Dohnavur. In his mother's opinion, harmony between him and Amy was impaired because Amy had been influenced by 'strong Plymouth Brethren nonconformism'.[14] Whatever the pejorative name was meant to cover, it had to include belief in the full inspiration of Scripture,

[13] Stephen Neill, *Anglicanism* (London: Penguin Books, 1960), p. 400.
[14] *Chance to Die*, p. 269.

or 'Fundamentalism', as that belief was now being classified.

What was actually discussed between Stephen Neill and Amy, now fifty-eight, has not been recorded. The twenty-five-year old graduate may have reminded her that the Church Missionary Society had declined to make the full inspiration of Scripture a necessary qualification for their missionaries. The presence of a 'new evangelicalism' had come fully into the open in 1922 when H. E. Fox and the Bible League had asked missionary societies not to send out to the mission field 'any who deny or doubt that every writing of the Old and New Testaments is God-breathed, through men who spoke from God, being moved by the Holy Ghost'.[15] The CMS offered no such assurance. This was not irrelevant for, as already noted, the society owned the original Dohnavur property. On July 6, 1925, after painful, sleepless nights, Amy withdrew from the Church of England Zenana Missionary

[15] Quoted by Andrew Atherstone in *Evangelicalism and Fundamentalism in the United Kingdom During the Twentieth Century*, eds. D. Bebbington and D. C. Jones (Oxford Universtity Press, 2013), p. 62.

Society which was linked with CMS. 'A dreadful time of distress', she wrote in her diary. 'Never such known here before.' She believed that 'the spiritual fortunes of the work hung by a thread'.[16] In August she wrote to a friend, 'I do trust that no one will ever know how difficult things are now.'

The crisis continued until November 1925 when Stephen Neill's continuance became impossible. On the 28th of that month Amy noted, 'One of the very saddest nights of my life.' The next day he was asked to leave.

Amy makes no reference at all to the Neills in her history of Dohnavur as given in *Gold Cord*, and the same silence is preserved in the Houghton biography. In this there was kindness on her part, and perhaps an element of churchmanship on the part of Houghton for, by the time his biography of Amy Carmichael was published, Stephen Neill was a bishop. Years later Elisabeth Elliot was right to break the silence, for the point at issue affected not only Dohnavur but the whole scene of world missions as I will seek to point out in

[16] *Chance to Die*, p. 268.

chapter 7 below. It is arguable that Dohnavur was to retain the old evangelical orthodoxy after Amy's death because there was no supervisory direction from London. The CMS allowed the mission station which they had originated, and which she had built up, to become independent.

It would be a misreading of this trouble to attribute it to any bias on Amy's part against the Church of England. Numbers of her friends belonged to that denomination. When the crisis was over, a new building became the place of worship in 1927. Without pictures, stained glass windows, or symbols, it became the place for three services every Sunday, one English and two Tamil. The Bishop of Tinnevelly was asked to take part in the opening. Explaining her thinking, Amy wrote:

> When the local bishop has been a friend whose coming would help towards the spiritual life of our company, we have asked him to come to us from time to time, and when he was not we have not.

After Neill became Bishop of Tinnevelly in 1939 he was not invited to Dohnavur.

In 1927 what had been formally known as the 'Dohnavur Nurseries' was formed on a legal basis as the Dohnavur Fellowship. The stated aim was,

> To save children in moral danger; to train them to serve others; to succour the desolate and the suffering; to do anything that may be shown to be the will of our Heavenly Father, in order to make His love known, especially to the people of India.

A council made up of eight of Amy's best helpers was formed, with no distinction made on grounds of nationality. Amy continued in the overall leadership of the work she had been given to do. The partings thus led to a real consolidation. Harmony had to rest on foundational beliefs. In the words of Elisabeth Ellliot:

> Three things mattered: the verbal inspiration of Scripture, the power of God to deal with His enemy, and loyalty to one another.

From this date there came a more careful scrutiny of candidates. A series of twenty-five questions would be put to volunteers, intended to avoid future disappointments, and to show that

Dohnavur would not be a comfortable place for all comers. These questions included:

> Samuel Rutherford said that there are some who would have Christ cheap, Christ 'without the cross. But the price will not come down.' Will you pay the price to live a crucified life?

> Besides the Bible, which three or four books have helped you the most? Besides reading books, what activity refreshes you best when tired?[17]

The late 1920s Amy came to regard as something like golden years. The staff situation had been greatly helped by the coming of two brothers, Murray Webb-Peploe,[18] along with his brother Godfrey, men of the same heartbeat as Amy. Murray, a doctor, took the leadership in the

---

[17] Amy was deeply persuaded of the importance of Christian literature. 'Send books', she would write home. The biographies of such missionaries as Henry Martyn and Adoniram Judson she regarded as 'a sort of standing dose of mental and spiritual quinine'. She had no time for fiction except in her later invalid days when she enjoyed the stories of John Buchan.

[18] Katharine Makower, *Follow My Leader: A biography of Murray Webb-Peploe including his years of service with Amy Carmichael at Dohnavur* (Eastbourne: Kingsway, 1984).

hospital, assisted by May Powell, while Godfrey met the urgent need for someone to head the work among the boys. It was a role for which he was ideally suited.

The addition of people and buildings did not mean as much to Amy as the evidence of the on-going work of God in their midst. Her dream that the babies and infant girls of earlier years would become 'mothers' and nurses of the next generation was being fulfilled. She saw that the long-term future lay with Indian leadership. For the present her plan was for May Powell to become the leader on the women's side, and the Webb-Peploe brothers on the men's.

I have sought in this chapter to highlight some leading events from two decades. The danger in doing so is that the humdrum events of ordinary life are too much out of view. What Amy wrote of Walker was true of herself. She was

> called to live a holy life—not in the ease of religious seclusion, nor in the midst of those rare heroic circumstances which emphasize the glory side of existence, but along the dusty levels of commonplace ways.

Other sentences in the Foreword to her biography of Walker speak of the kind of daily routine in which she worked:

> Always there were hindrances, just simple and ordinary: the crush of other duties around one, the impossibility of assured quiet for even an hour at a stretch, the lack of invigorating influences—for who finds the Plains of India invigorating?

then she added words which epitomize the story of her life, 'But I have been splendidly helped.'

Her books were a vital feature of this whole period. Between *Things as They Are* in 1903 to *Gold Cord* in 1932, some seventeen other items had come from her pen, of various shapes and sizes, *Walker of Tinnevelly* at 458 pages being the largest. The necessity for the help of those who would pray had initiated this flow of literature but it also came to have another purpose. Initially, while Robert Wilson of Keswick was alive,[19] additional financial support was not as

---

[19] He had died in 1905, and was buried in the small Quaker burial ground in the fields above his home at Broughton Grange. A simple stone bears the words, 'All one in Christ Jesus' (*Gal.* 3:28). Dohnavur was a

urgent as it would later become, but the books brought a world-wide circle of friends, and by 1923 there were seven volunteer secretaries representing Dohnavur. Irene Streeter of Oxford followed Catherine Carmichael in that role in England, others were in Co. Wicklow, Ireland; Dunlop, Scotland; Melbourne, Australia; Christ Church, New Zealand; Albany, USA; Ontario, Canada. All were asked 'to restrain from asking for gifts' and there was to be 'no collection at any meeting'.[20]

The work at Dohnavur inevitably brought visitors. In 1910 Amy could speak of as many as 65 unexpected guests arriving. Her correspondents came to be a much larger number, with letters arriving from many more countries than those named above.

---

testimony to the truth of the text.

[20] *Tables in the Wilderness*, p. 153. This book of 151 pages details something of the financial side of the work. Dohnavur was not a 'faith' mission in the sense of not making the needs of the work known, but Amy was cautious and endorsed the words of Hudson Taylor: 'The apostolic plan was not to raise ways and means but to go and do the work, trusting his promise who said, "Seek ye first the kingdom of God and his righteousness and all these things shall be added unto you."'

If some of her correspondents thought of Dohnavur as 'a kind of Garden of Eden without the serpent', she was quick to disabuse them.[21] Visitors to Dohnavur might admire the harmony there but, as we have seen, times of strife and tension were not unknown, As Walker would say, 'The perfect church, not having spot or blemish or any such thing is yet to come.' Heaven is not yet.

[21] *Houghton*, p. 257.

11. Amy in 1925, aged 57.

12. Boys with Amma's dog.

13. By the Red Lake.

14. Girls in the 1940s.

15. Boys observing the bullock-bandy.

16. On their way to the forest.

17. The House of Prayer.

18. Part of the Dohnavur buildings.

19. Memorial to Amy Carmichael at Dohnavur.

5

THE 1930s AND 1940s

Gone, they tell me, is youth,
Gone is the strength of my life,
Nothing remains but decline,
Nothing but age and decay.

Not so, I'm God's little child,
Only beginning to live;
Coming the days of my prime,
Coming the strength of my life,
Coming the vision of God,
Coming my bloom and my power.[1]

A.C. 1935

[1] *Gold by Moonlight*, p. 177.

At the age of sixty-three Amy suffered an accident which, physically at least, meant a transition from one life to another. On the morning of October 24, 1931, she had prayed, 'Do with me as Thou wilt. Do anything that will fit me to serve Thee and help my beloveds.' A normal day followed until the late afternoon when she went the five or six miles to a Muslim and Hindu town where they were preparing facilities for a medical dispensary. As she examined building work which was being done, she entered a half-finished hut in the twilight and fell into a pit which was being dug for a toilet in the wrong place. She broke her leg, dislocated an ankle and twisted her spine.

For a period there was hope that Amy might be restored to health and a log book noted her seeming progress: 'Amma walked six steps'; 'Amma walked ten steps'; 'A. carried to prayer room for meeting'; 'A. stood for short spells'; 'first night without pain mobility', and so on. But a recovery of mobility was not to be. The toll of 36 uninterrupted years in India had weakened her constitution. Neuritis and arthritis set in and she could rarely sleep without medication. There would be no more 'whizzing' about the compound, or climbing in the forests and mountains. Apart from an occasional car outing, and a September visit to the Forest home, life would now be spent very largely in her room. Instead of the open air she loved, she would look more at the painting of the majestic Nanga Parbat peak, hanging on her wall, and at the birds in the veranda aviary just outside her window. Short walks in the garden beyond would be the most she could usually do.

Yet there was no question of any retirement, and, as Frank Houghton has written, except for the times of more acute suffering, her mental activity was such as would have made heavy demands on 'much younger and healthier people'. The well-being of everyone within the family remained her chief interest. Hours would be spent daily talking to staff members, or to children who wanted to see her. Difficult children could have her particular attention. Through most of the years which followed she wrote a short daily message to the whole family with some scriptural truth and often bearing on the necessity of unity. The words of John Buchan on Cromwell were meaningful to her: 'He strove to give his command so strict a unity that in no crisis should it crack.' It was the need for constant watchfulness against disunity that prompted her little book, *If*. It began with the words:

> If I have not compassion on my fellow-servant, even as my Lord has pity on me, then I know nothing of Calvary love.

Trouble could also arise between the children, as when some wanted to stand apart from those they supposed born illegitimately. There were those who were simply rebellious, no matter how much they were cared for.

Finding the best staff would also remain a constant care. Stephen Neill was not the last one to be dismissed. In 1937 she would speak of 'the painful breaking up of hopes and expectations', when it was discovered that two trusted helpers had been long acting with 'deceit and disobedience'. Their instant removal brought objections from others and criticism from supporters at a distance. It was a 'crashing sorrow' which, she feared, 'undid the work of years'.[1]

For the most part, certainly, it was the harmony at Dohnavur which impressed visitors. One Indian worker in the family for many years has spoken of the strains which could arise from female leadership. When Elisabeth Elliot asked him, if most of the men found it difficult to work under female authority, 'One hundred per cent of them', was his reply. 'But the women?' 'Never, in all my wanderings, have I seen thirty or forty women live together in such harmony as I saw in the Dohnavur Fellowship.'[2]

Dr Murray Webb-Peploe, and his brother Godfrey, are not to be included in the 'one hundred percent' named in the above statement. For them, Amy was a friend and 'mother' rather than an employer. They understood and loved her, and were mainstays in the work, Murray

[1] See *Chance to Die*, p. 334.
[2] *Ibid.*, p. 284.

until he had to return to England in 1947 and Godfrey until his death at Dohnavur two years later. The sheer size of the work was bound to produce problems. By the 1940s there were some 900 children and grown-ups, including between forty and fifty helpers. The hospital work grew to such an extent that a medical superintendent was needed, as well as three doctors. The man first appointed to that post proved too authoritarian in his dealing with Indian people. It was out of harmony with what was needed for the continuance of the work and he did not stay.

One of the things which brought children and others to Amy's room was to borrow books. Here were the bookcases, Amy has written,

> to which the household would come when they want biography, missionary and otherwise, and books of other kinds too. They are my great luxury, my mental change of air.

Her enthusiasm for 'old' rather than modern books must have touched some of them. The old for her were like 'wells' of cool refreshment, while the modern, in comparison, could be 'sawdust', 'thin', 'skimmed milk and tepid tea'.

* * *

Amy's accident and confinement after 1931 brought something further into her ministry of writing. Before that date, she could say, 'The mere thought of indoor life was anathema to me.' When the dramatic change came she knew the lessons to be practised: 'You must never ask God why?' 'To will what God wills brings peace.' The school of suffering became the richest school of her life, and in it, as Frank Houghton says, 'Christ gave her words which could not have been written apart from that experience.' Her book titles in the earlier years had dealt with missionary subjects or the work at Dohnavur. Among the thirteen books produced after her accident, there were to be seven on what it means to live with Christ in all the circumstances of trials of life. In these she wrote not of her own experience but out of it. The first of these seven was *Rose from Brier* (1933), of which Ruth Graham has written, 'As pain is not always physical, it is a book for all who suffer. It is by far the best that I have found.' Of wider compass and appeal is the title already quoted in these pages, *Gold by Moonlight* (1935). Its themes were prompted by fine photographs sent to her by a friend who had been in the Austrian Tyrol and the Bavarian Alps. In the scenes depicted, Amy saw pictures of what all believers are likely to experience, 'The Dark Wood', 'The Ravine', 'Rough Waters', 'The Shining Summit', and much more. The book's title was drawn from Samuel Rutherford's words, 'It is possible to gather gold, where it may be had, with moonlight.' The book, she told the readers, was for 'any who are walking in difficult places and who care to gather that gold'.

Although moonlight is not sunshine, it well suits those who walk by faith, not by sight. And faith is the key to the Christian's happiness:

> We in our lesser mystery
> Of lingering ill and winged death,
> Would fain see clear, but, could we see,
> What need would be for faith?[3]

No air of gloom came from Amy's sick room. Sadness involves disbelief in the love of God. Whatever the trials they are not greater than the love. So in another poem, 'The World is Bright',

[3] *Dohnavur Songs*, p. 81.

she writes,

> Though it be true
> Who loveth suffereth too,
> Do not love's tender, joyful gains
> Far more than balance all life's pains?
> We know they do.[4]

Houghton has noted that *Rose from Brier* and *Gold by Moonlight*, were both read by more than 20,000 and 'evoked more letters of appreciation than almost any others of Amma's books'.[5] Of the 1930s, he further writes:

> There was a tremendous increase in the number of Christian people throughout the world who were deeply moved by the challenge of her books. I think it is true to say that God used her pen for more widespread and deeper

[4] *Ibid.*, p. 17. Amy was heartily in accord with words of Billy Bray. Present in a fellowship meeting of Cornish believers, he heard several speak of how their trials were counterbalanced by blessings. But after listening a while he thought the testimonies were not strong enough, and he told the gathering, 'Well friends, I have been taking vinegar and honey, but praise the Lord, I've had the vinegar with a *spoon*, but the honey with a *ladle*.' F. W. Bourne, *The King's Son: or, Memoir of Billy Bray* (London: Bible Christian, 1887), p. 29.

[5] *Houghton*, p. 334.

spiritual blessing during the post-accident period than in all the preceding years.

Most if not all of Amy's history of Dohnavur, *Gold Cord* (1932) was written before her accident which is not mentioned. She was reluctant to write any continuation of that history and questioned her ability to do it. Then, in her notebook for July 1936, she recorded the conviction that it was something she was being given to do:

> Suddenly on the morning of the 24th (after a poor night) I felt I was to do it, and could do it. Worked without stopping that day and the next—about thirteen hours each day—and on the 26th the same except for two breaks. Cannot account for it on any natural ground, as nothing is different. Lord and Master of my life, Owner of every minute, I thank Thee.

The book came out with the title *Windows* in 1937.

The wider circulation of her books necessarily entailed an increased correspondence from many lands. In the 1930s Frank Houghton could speak of her dealing with 'thousands' of letters in both English and Tamil. Commenting on the circulation of her titles down to 1953, Houghton noted that it was only in rare cases that less than 10,000 copies were printed, and that 'There are nine books in "the 15,000 and over" category.' It is very probable that circulation figures increased considerably after 1953. The Carmichael title, *Edges of His Ways* (1955), put together by a friend after her death, was reprinted four times by 1964 to the extent of 42,952 copies.

It is not clear whether Houghton is referring only to books in English. Her writing to that date had been translated into fifteen languages, including Tamil and four other Indian tongues. Twelve of her titles were also produced in Braille for the National Library for the Blind in England, and eight for the Braille Circulating Library in the United States.[6]

Natural gifts for writing Amy Carmichael undoubtedly had, yet they might have remained dormant if, in coming to India, she was not stirred to write 'words of fire'. 'Writing is torn from a person,' it has been said. 'If you are going

---

[6] Houghton's chapter on 'Amy as Author' is one of his best.

to say something worthwhile, you're going to burn.' Amy's thirty-five books, born of prayer, are in that category. Whether they relate to what she saw in South India, or to the Christian life in general, they were written because she had a message. 'Pray', she noted for the family,

> that every book, booklet, letter, that goes out from this Fellowship may have blood and iron in it. Pray that we may never degenerate to the merely interesting.

We do not wonder at the sale of her books. It is compulsive writing which leads to compulsive reading.

From 1928 SPCK in London were her leading publishers, she consulted with them over every detail on her titles with the result that the hardbacks stood out in the beauty of their appearance. 'Dowdiness', she believed, 'is not acceptable to the Lord of beauty.' A hint she gave to a would-be author reflected her own care: 'Words should be like colours, each one supplying a dot of colour supplying a need, not one over.' This is not to say that her style appeals to every Christian, and her use of imagination may at times be overdone. There is poetry and art in her language yet, as Houghton says, 'the very quality which lifted and inspired so many made her seem obscure to others'.

* * *

The 1940s were much the same as the previous decade as far as Amy's personal life was concerned. Dohnavur was far removed from the troubles of the Second World War, although that was not certain in 1942 when there was possibility of a Japanese invasion of India. Plans were prepared in case an evacuation of numbers from the compound would be advisable. Although Amy's location was remote, she was familiar with newspapers and magazines which came regularly from Europe. She maintained an active interest in world news, and doubted whether Hitler should be prayed for.

After the war the scene changed and a call for India's independence came to the fore. Amy did not favour it, not because of any permanent rule she claimed for Britain, but because she believed the country was not ready. It was a belief shared by some Indians. When India ceased to be part of the British Empire on August 14, 1947, the bloodshed and massacres, which followed the partition of the land between Hindus and Muslims, justified the misgivings. But Amy had long believed that the future of the work in Dohnavur would lie in the hands of Indian Christians. In 1938 she had written that the helpers sought from overseas needed to 'believe as we do that India can best be reached by Indians'.

With that in mind, the preparation of chosen women for leadership was very much part of her vision. Such friends as Kohila and Arulia were as close to her as any sister; she looked to them for the future of the work, and their unexpected deaths were a trial to her. She knew that all things could not be, and should not be ever as in her day. Elisabeth Elliot believed that 'she really tried to turn over the reins to others', but, 'The time for cutting apron strings never seemed to arise.'[7] By 1950 the needed change could not be delayed. Of the three deputy leaders of 1931, with the Webb-Peploe brothers gone, only one remained.

[7] *Chance to Die*, p. 345.

Accordingly Dohnavur had its first two Indians, Rajappan and Purripu, brought into the leadership group. Amy's confidence for the future was that Christ would be with the race she loved.

> When decisions have to be made, don't look back and wonder what I would have done. Look up, and light will come to show what our Lord and Master would have you do.[8]

A fall in her room in 1948 meant a virtual end of movement for the last two and a half years of Amy's life. There were long sleepless nights and five months when 'pain held sway night and day'. Even so, she sought to fill in 'the crevices of time'. In 1949, while writing had to give way to dictation, praying did not cease. 'Let us die climbing' had long been her desire.

Beyond her room, the lives of the now 900 children and helpers went on. In Elisabeth Elliot's words:

> Rice, by the ton, was pounded by hand, parboiled in great pots, cooked daily, and eaten. Babies were fed, bathed and changed and rocked and sung to and carried out to play.

[8] *Chance to Die*, p. 345.

Bottles were prepared, diapers washed, nurseries scrubbed, walks swept, tiles and brass vessels polished, gardens weeded. The children bathed under the pumps, ate their curries, learned their lessons. The bells of the Prayer Tower called the Family to prayer and rang out the evening hymn.[9]

Some of these sounds reached Amy. They found her, when she was turned eighty, revising her *Walker of Tinnevelly*. Her thoughts went back to the day Preena fled to her arms; to the red earth, and the old cottage, where infants slept on the veranda before there were any nurseries at Dohnavur; to times, too, when all might have been wrecked. What was of God, she knew, would last. When her faith was challenged, as it still was, she urged herself and her colleagues, 'Let us rise to this great trust.'

Amy's room in her last years must not be thought of simply as a place of pain and shadows. There were many times of laughter. Once when a helper of forty years earlier came to visit, she acted the Amy she had seen her then, shaking her head, brushing back a wisp of hair with her

[9] *Ibid.*, p. 354

hand, and questioning, 'Art thou an elephant to walk so slowly?' As Amy later reported the sketch, she was represented,

> not walking nor even running but *flying*, with many a glance at a wristlet watch 'lest we waste moments' (I had no idea I had that absurd habit, but I saw it now, and the two or three of us who were her audience shook with laughter as we watched the pantomime).[10]

A mournful life was far from Amy's conception of what a Christian's ought to be. To one of her nurses, about to leave on furlough, she said, 'We won't meet again in this world. When you hear I have gone, jump for joy.' One of her last dictated letters included the words, 'I am very happy and content. Green pastures are before me, and my Saviour has my treasure—the DF.'

Her 83rd birthday came and passed on December 16, 1950. Then the day she awaited came on the morning of January 18, 1951, and the Prayer Tower rang out the tune of a favourite hymn, 'Ten Thousand Times Ten Thousand.' Back on June 21, 1900—her arrival date at the future

---

[10] *Houghton*, p. 293.

home—the place had resounded with song. So it was at her departure. 'She was', as one remembered her, 'happy hearted, never gloomy, lively in worship, festive in rejoicing. She wanted joy, triumph, tambourines, even after burial.'

Amy Carmichael, according to her instructions, was buried in the garden beyond her windows. It was 'God's Garden', for here were the babies, children, and grown-ups who had gone before. There was to be no memorial stone. None was needed, for her memory would be guarded by love, and the grave was only temporary:

> And when Jesus comes what then
>   They will rise again
> They will rise as flower from the seed
>   That was dead indeed
> But quickened by secret power
>   Has awaked a flower
> They will rise and rise and rise
>   And meet our Lord in the skies.[11]

> A.C.

[11] *Paper Book and Selected Songs*, item 170.

20. Tree at the entrance to 'God's Garden', Dohnavur.

6

THE LIFE AND ITS MESSAGE

Shadow and shine art Thou,
  Dear Lord, to me;
Pillar of cloud and fire,
  I follow Thee.
What though the way be long,
  In Thee my heart is strong,
Thou art my joy, and song—
  Praise, praise to Thee.

A.C.

In her biography of Thomas Walker, Amy Carmichael set down a warning she sought to observe. Walker, she tells us, after reading a life of a good man, said that it was spoiled by 'too much paint'. And she commented, 'In India we do not paint our teak: we let it show its grain: teak asks for no pretence.'[1] The opinion has been expressed that Amy's own biographers, Houghton and Elliot, did not keep this in mind.

Dr Gaius Davies, a present-day author, in using a metaphor different from paint, believes that, while the portrayal of her life by these biographers is 'a great help', 'both writers are at times brought down by what one might call a "Dohnavur virus". By this I mean that critical appraisal and careful assessment are exchanged for a kind of hero-worship which is not very helpful.'[2]

[1] *Walker of Tinnevelly*, p. v.
[2] *Genius, Grief & Grace, A Doctor Looks at Suffering*

Certainly, an assessment of Amy Carmichael as a person is not straightforward. If certain features of her life are highlighted and others passed over, it is possible to come away with a distorted portrait. There is in her an intense spiritual note which, taken alone, might warrant Dr Davies' epithet of 'the mother superior'. But there was also a very human side. 'She had', said one who knew her, 'a sense of humour, which saved the day many a time'.[3] One young doctor, newly arrived at Dohnavur, wrote of her first impression:

> There was a lightness, brightness and joy about her. She was loving, lovely and warm. Not much over five feet, I suspect, with grey hair, wearing a blue *sari*. She had a twinkle, a gentle sense of humour.[4]

There are other instances, which Elliot has recorded, which show she was no 'plaster saint'. An old Irish temper could surface on occasion. When she was told of a scene in which someone

---

and Success (Fearn, Ross-shire: Christian Focus, 2001), p. 241.

[3] *Follow My Leader*, p. 127.

[4] *Chance to Die*, p. 304.

had behaved badly, she exclaimed, 'If I had been there I should have torn up a bush by the roots and laid on like a fishwife. But then I am not a pacifist.' On another occasion she so disagreed with a friend at dinner that she told him she felt like throwing the plate of soup at him!

In estimating how much weight is given to reflections on her life, attention needs to be given to the date when they were expressed. Houghton was three times at Dohnavur, in the 1930s and '40s. Elisabeth Elliott never met Amy but was in close contact with members of the Dohnavur Fellowship before writing her biography of 1987.

Elliot gives examples of how some who criticized Amy in her lifetime were to change their opinion on meeting her and seeing the work. An Indian pastor, hearing reports of the Fellowship from a distance, concluded the children were brought up 'like hot house plants'. When he met her, he was ashamed of his prejudice:

> My doubts vanished. Instinctively I felt that here was a person just beside me who had realized God. I have never seen such a beautiful face.

A Canadian woman psychiatrist went to visit, expecting to garner an interesting case study of a neurotic old lady. Five minutes convinced the doctor she has picked the wrong lady.[5]

When Amy was asked to speak to a house meeting in Madras, a group came to hear her in which there were similar prejudices, including dislike of a British woman wearing Indian dress. In the thinking of some of them, she was a 'dreamer' and her opening words, 'I had a dream last night', confirmed their estimate. But not for long. She began:

> I had a dream last night. I thought I had come to this gathering, and an aged child of God with many years' service behind him was asked to pray. 'O Lord', he said, 'here we are gathered together for yet another meeting, and Thou knowest how tired we are of such meetings. Help us to get through this one.'

At this, Houghton reports, 'The frozen atmosphere melted, and a ripple of laughter spread over the audience.'[6]

[5] *Chance to Die*, p. 329.
[6] *Houghton*, p. 184.

Certainly there were elements in Amy's make-up which might seem contradictory. She avoided the limelight, wrote the history of Dohnavur with scarce a reference to herself, tried to avoid an honour conferred by the government,[7] and insisted on no gravestone for her memory; yet one visitor at Dohnavur wrote, 'There was only one boss and that was Amma. She wouldn't proceed with any course of action until everyone had agreed, but who dared oppose her?'

Part of the explanation must lie in the circumstances. After the death of Walker in 1912, there was no one else to share in leadership and, for years to come, no one was her equal in gifts and wisdom. One who became a friend in 1916, and was of similar ability, was Dr Eleanor McDougall, 'who argued with her and chaffed her as

[7] A few years after the First World War, the Governor of Madras informed her that she was included in the Royal Birthday Honours and was to receive a medal. Consternation was her response. 'I have done nothing to make it fitting and cannot understand it at all.' *Ibid.*, p. 236.

few others could do'.[8] But McDougall lived in Madras and was only occasionally at Dohnavur. By the time a team of competent helpers had become established, Amy was so far ahead in terms of experience in what was predominantly a women's work, that her leadership was the most natural thing. If it had been effectively challenged by the Neill family in 1924–25, it would not have been to the betterment of the work. She saw herself as put in a role not chosen by herself. She had come to India to be an assistant evangelist, not an Amma to generations of children. A sense of calling was fundamental to her life.

The pride present in fallen human nature still troubles Christians, and Amy did not regard herself as exempt. But there is evidence of its mortification. No photographs of herself appeared in books published in her lifetime. She did not have the aversion to criticism which marks those desirous of preeminence. In a preface to one of

[8] *Houghton*, p. 193. It was McDougall, Houghton says, who introduced Amy to the mystic writers, such as St Theresa, believing that she could 'sift the pure wheat' from 'the chaff'. If Amy was to recommend those writers I am not aware of it.

her books she referred to criticism 'fair and perhaps sometimes otherwise', and said of the book,

> As it goes out again, it goes out with prayer for forgiveness for anything amiss in it, and with longing that it might help some young soul (it was not written for old souls) a little nearer its goal.[9]

At the same time there is a feature which needs fuller comment. She is criticised for being over-confident of her own judgment in matters of guidance and unwilling to defer to others. In so far as such a trait arose from her long experience of the work, it is understandable. But sometimes more was involved and the manner in which she came to decisions needs some consideration. She believed that definite guidance on a course of action to be taken might be received from God, and that this could be through a verse of Scripture strongly impressed on the mind. This was direction different from the type of guidance gained only from general biblical principles and prayerful reflection. It rested on a particular verse

[9] *God's Missionary* (London: SPCK, 1939). This book was in its tenth reprint by 1953.

which was to be understood to mean something other than the meaning in the original context. So Robert Wilson was serious in using the direction Paul gave to Timothy, 'Do thy diligence to come to me before winter' (2 *Tim.* 4:9), to enlighten Amy on her duty to return from Ceylon to England in 1894.[10]

Examples of this use of Scripture for guidance occur in the Dohnavur story. When a decision had to be made on whether or not money currently available should be spent on purchasing land for a new hospital building, Amy felt that it should. But much weight was put on the words of Joshua 3:15, 'As they that bear the ark were come to Jordan, and the feet of the priests that bare the ark were dipped in the brim of the water ...' The relevance of the text she understood in this way: 'dipped' meant 'plunged', and it meant they were to take 'the plunge of faith'.

The money went to the hospital building, but Christian experience has shown that it is a hazardous business to determine a course of action

[10] It would appear that D.O.M. used the text with Amy more than once after she left England; she said it was 'like a knife thrust'. *Chance to Die*, p. 326.

on such a basis. Where guidance is supposed to have been received in this way, with God's sanction claimed for it, an unwillingness to have it questioned can naturally follow. This feature did appear in Amy. Yet it is wrong to assert, as some have done, that she never changed her mind or accepted the opinion of others on what should be done.[11] In fairness to her it must also be said that, for her, guidance was primarily a matter of prayer and waiting on God, as well as looking to Scripture. As she matured she was increasingly aware of the danger of being led by mere subjective feelings, and that presumption can lie close to faith. In the 1930s she opposed the teaching of the Oxford Group movement who claimed that 'direct guidance' is given to the person in whom there is complete surrender.[12]

---

[11] For an example, see *Ibid.*, pp. 362-3.

[12] *Houghton*, p. 300. Her impetuous going to Ceylon in 1894 was defended by the words, 'One dare not do anything but obey when that Voice speaks.' But we have no infallible way to discern between feelings of our own and a 'voice of God'. When Amy was rightly advised in the 1940s that the old Ford car needed replacing, she said she did not 'feel' it right to buy a new one. Soon after, when the car's brakes failed in a hazardous

Another example of the use of Scripture for a purpose other than its original intention, was Amy's belief that the calling of a missionary is as distinct and irrevocable as the vow to be taken by a Nazarite. The words of Numbers 6:2-4 are prefixed prominently to her little book, *God's Missionary*, and she writes, 'God's true missionary is a Nazarite, who has "made a special vow, the vow of one separated, to separate himself unto the LORD".' She speaks of the missionary calling as a 'special calling' which 'by its very nature, calls us apart from everything else'. It requires 'an entire separation and devotion to the work'.[13]

The emphasis she wanted to give in using these words was right; it is parallel to Paul's words in 2 Timothy 2:4. She was warning against what she had seen of missionary work in India, where too much time could go to recreations with fellow Europeans, and a too-ready acceptance of

situation, feelings did not need to be considered. As Elliot comments, tensions could arise at Dohnavur in 'conflicts between what Amma thought God wanted and what others thought God wanted'. *Chance to Die*, p. 350.

[13] *God's Missionary*. My quotations are from pp. 14, 6-7, 16.

such 'amusements' as novel reading. While she did not decry recreations as such (she enjoyed swimming), she believed that the spirituality necessary for vibrant Christian witness was being weakened by too many distractions and entanglement with lesser things. Her strictures were not without balance:

> We are variously made. What rests one person wearies another. The great thing is to find what rests us most, what sends us back to our work most truly refreshed in body, soul and spirit.[14]

Yet Amy's concern for single-mindedness did not justify the imposition of the Nazarite pattern, with its vow for perpetual separation, on missionaries. It was a pattern which could bring unhappy consequences. It could justify a missionary living apart from wife or children on account of a 'special' calling.[15] The highest devotion to

[14] *Ibid.*, p. 45. 'Our thought ... is not to define another's duty but to urge that each of us should be sincere in finding out our own.'

[15] An example of this tension occurred at Dohnavur after Oda, the wife of Murray Webb-Peploe, took their children back to England for schooling in 1945. Unable to cope on her own, Oda pleaded for her husband to

Christ is consistent with marital responsibility, and 'separation', rightly understood, is not obligatory for only a special class of believers.

To accept that Amy's handling of Scripture was at some points faulty, is not to say that there was some inherent weakness in all her treatment of Scripture. Far from it. She did not fall into the idiosyncrasies or errors which have marked some prominent Christian women. Nor did she follow any of the new ideas, which arose in her day, seeking the acceptance of the more 'spiritual' of evangelicals. For example, after the revival of 1905, the public confession of past sin by professing believers came to be widely promoted, and, in her words, 'tortured sensitive souls'. She agreed with Walker in opposing it:

---

follow her and make a home for their boys. But to him this seemed akin to abandoning the call he had known in 1928 and in this concern he was confirmed by Amy. It took Murray time to see that they were wrong and his wife was right. Years later he wrote wisely: 'God guides through thought (intuition), through the Bible and through circumstances. Each couple must get their own guidance from the Lord, and he is sovereign as to the outcome.' See Makower, *Follow My Leader*, pp. 155-60. David Livingstone virtually abandoned his wife, with sad consequences.

Confession of any sin which binds us and hinders us in the cause is a duty. But raking up the buried and pardoned sin of the past is not.

Nor does secret sin against God need public disclosure, rather 'the less people said about themselves the better', as John Newton referred to in his verse,

> When I would speak what Thou hast done
> To save me from my sin,
> I cannot make Thy mercies known,
> But self-applause comes in.[16]

She had the same discernment over what became known as 'faith healing'. It quickly had its advocates in India where the possibility of becoming a healer in the land of so much sickness had strong appeal. Numbers of people 'advised' her of how Dohnavur could become a centre of healing miracles if she learned the 'prayer of faith':

> We searched our Bibles then, to find our Lord's thought about this matter; and we read the scores of letters that came from the ends of the earth, each urging upon us some new view

[16] *Walker of Tinnevelly*, pp. 427-8.

of divine healing. There was a day when we asked Him, if He willed it so, to give us the gift, the *charisma*, that had been in apostolic times. Would it not glorify His name? And what joy it would be to see pain instantly relieved—for though we did see a putting forth of power, there was not anything comparable to the healing of the first century. The *charisma* was not given ... We know not what we should pray for as we ought. Not our poor thoughts, but the counsels of the Holy One, be our guide.[17]

Given the submission to the sovereignty of God which pervaded her life, the idea of 'claiming' anything from God was unthinkable. In that same connexion she wrote:

Our little children had taught us many things. We knew they did not always know what was good for them, and we should have been very grieved if they had persisted in imploring for something, after we had let them understand that we could not give it ... Not, 'Thy will be changed' but 'Thy will be done', is the prayer we are taught to pray.[18]

[17] *Gold Cord*, pp. 257-8.
[18] *Houghton*, p. 185.

This was not to conclude that God does not heal today. Sometimes he does. At Dohnavur 'there have been healings that nothing could account for but the presence of the Lord Jesus'.[19] But this was not by means of any miraculous healing gift, as in apostolic times, or by teaching the sick child or person to obtain healing by the 'prayer of faith'. On the contrary, Amy warned against such people as the specious faith healer, known to her, who induced 'vast numbers to vow that they would never go near a doctor'.

* * *

It is in the sphere of practical Christianity and living the Christian life that Amy Carmichael's help to us is strongest. While she understood that a right understanding of Scripture is foundational, it was the devotional application of a doctrine, rather than its exegesis, which drew her comments. So in writing on Ephesians 1:4, 'He chose us as His own ... before the creation of the world' (Weymouth), she proceeds in this characteristic way:

[19] *Gold Cord*, pp. 264-5.

Before 'the morning stars sang together and all the sons of God shouted for joy', He loved me, and 'chose me as His own'. Therefore today every spiritual blessing may be truly mine—the ninefold fruit of the Spirit, love, joy, peace, patience towards others, kindness, goodness (that sweetness of heart that was Christ's), good faith, meekness, self-restraint—so that in the pressure of life I need not fail. And all this is 'to the praise of the glory of His grace'.[20]

Two main features stand out both in Amy Carmichael's life and in her writings.

The first is the place of quietness in the life of the Christian.

I do not think there is anything from the beginning of our Christian life to the end, that is so keenly attacked as our quiet with God, for it is in quietness that we are fed.[21]

This was a need she had noted early in her Christian life. She never forgot the crowded tent at the Keswick Convention where there was 'Wave after wave of silent prayer, rising solemnly to God.' Services of worship with the children at

[20] *Edges of His Ways*, p. 57.
[21] *Ibid.*, p. 34.

Dohnavur began with a minute of silence, and even in the busiest of her days it was her habit to pause and look at the calm of the hills above.

This grace matured in her after the accident of 1931. We can well believe that the confinement which she would not have chosen deepened her understanding of being 'quiet towards God'. Increasingly, for her, prayer is worship and adoration.

> In the hush of that nearness we shall not seek anything for ourselves, not even help, or light, or comfort; we shall forget ourselves, 'lost in wonder, love and praise'.[22]

> To pray in a hurry of spirit means nothing. ... There is nothing creative in noise. To live in a hurry means to do much but effect little.[23]

Her own prayer was,

> My Father, quiet me,
> Till in Thy holy presence, hushed,
> I think Thy thoughts with Thee.[24]

---

[22] *Ibid.*, p. 56.
[23] *Gold by Moonlight*, p. 112.
[24] *Dohnavur Songs*, item 99.

In another verse she wrote,

> Jesus, Lord of quiet ...
> With adoring wonder,
> I would seek Thy face.[25]

From this fellowship with God, faith was fed, and she learned to 'accept the unexplainable ... the delays, the disappointments and reverses'.

The second feature of her life was love. If there is a predominant concern in her writing it is the desire to help Christians raise their standard of discipleship by living more closely to God. This she did, not by promoting some special teaching, or instruction in rules to practice, but by showing how love is foundational to being a Christian.[26] Devotion to Christ belongs to the terms of being

---

[25] *Dohnavur Songs*, item 162.

[26] 'Some years ago, I surveyed the entire New Testament looking for instances where various Christian character traits were taught by precept or by example. I found twenty-seven. It may not surprise you that *love* was taught most often, some fifty times. It may surprise you that *humility* was a close second with forty instances. But what really surprised me is that *trust in God* in all our circumstances was third, being taught thirteen or more times.' Jerry Bridges, *Respectable Sins: Confronting the Sins We Tolerate* (NavPress, 2007), p. 63.

a disciple: 'If any man will come after me, let him deny himself, and take up his cross daily, and follow me. For whosoever will save his life shall lose it: but whosoever will lose his life for my sake, the same will save it' (*Luke* 9:23-4). But love in us starts on God's side: 'We love him because he first loved us' (*1 John* 4:19). The gift of a new nature in the rebirth is the cause of love: 'Let us love one another: for love is of God; and every one that loves is born of God and knows God' (*1 John* 4:7).

The strength of the emphasis in Amy Carmichael's life and writing lies in God's love to us in Christ. The more we know of his love, the less we shall think about self at all.

> All our love flows from His heart of love. We are like little pools on the rocks at Joppa. You know how we have watched the great sea washing over them and flooding them till they overflow. That is what the love of God does for us. We have no love in ourselves, and our pools would soon be empty if it were not for that great, glorious, exhaustless sea of love.[27]

[27] *Houghton*, p. 348. Joppa, a place on the coast to which the children were taken. See above, p. 80.

Love through me, Love of God,
Make me like Thy clear air
That Thou dost pour Thy colours through,
As though it were not there.

To abide in his love is the key to all:

If love weakens among us, if it ever becomes possible to tolerate the least shadow of an unloving thought, our Fellowship will begin to perish. Unlove is deadly. It is a cancer. It may kill slowly but it always kills in the end … If unlove is discovered anywhere, stop everything and put it right, if possible at once.[28]

Nothing is sweeter than love; nothing stronger, nothing higher, nothing broader, nothing more pleasant, nothing fuller or better in heaven and in earth; for love is born of God, and can rest only in God above all things created.

Love is the answer to all things: love ends all questions. Lord, ever more give us this love.[29]

Amy Carmichael seldom said anything about herself, and she had no thought of having attained to what she believed:

---

[28] *Houghton*, p. 219.
[29] Amy Carmichael, *God's Missionary*, pp. 57-8.

Don't think I am that myself! I fall far short of my own standard. But that is what I want to be, and that is what we must be if we are to stand the strain and conquer.[30]

Her use of the prayer of Jeremy Taylor was life-long:

Lord, do Thou turn me all into love, and all my love into obedience, and let my obedience be without interruption.

How she saw herself and how others saw her, were two very different things. She was unconscious of the first part of the description that Frank Houghton wrote of her: 'She loved much, and she is greatly loved.' He went on to say,

Dear Amma—she never understood how the love of God within her was so powerful a magnet that all through her life others were drawn irresistibly to her.[31]

For Amy enthusiasm is love on fire: 'Many waters cannot quench love, neither can the floods drown it' (*Song of Sol.* 8:7). Love is no anaemic thing. It is indignant and makes a Christian bold

[30] *Chance to Die*, p. 197.
[31] *Houghton*, p. 105.

in the presence of evil. It gives rise to zeal for the honour of God, and to a selfless regard for others. Having its source in the indwelling of Christ, by faith in that indwelling the Christian's capacity to love is enlarged (*Eph.* 3:17-19). 'As love grows we discover further and further the capacity of the house of our soul.'[32] Closer attachment to Christ is the great message of Amy Carmichael's writings. A glimpse of what that meant to her we can see in the closing words of her book *Gold by Moonlight*:

> What will it be to see Him whom I have known so long but never seen before? To adore His beauty, to worship Him in holiness; to see Him crowned with glory and honour who was wounded, bruised, oppressed, afflicted—what will it be to see Him and not another, not a stranger? What will it be to serve in perfect purity and in untiring vigour? To see no more through a glass darkly, to grope no more on the edge of knowledge, but to press

[32] Amy would have valued the words of B. B. Warfield in a sermon on Ephesians 3:14-19: 'The Spirit works love, and only through working this love, enlarges our apprehension. Love is the great enlarger.' *Faith and Life* (Edinburgh: Banner of Truth, 1990), p. 275.

on into that kingdom to which no frontier is set? To see with new eyes, to hear with new ears, to know no more in part but even as also we are known?

What will it be when Faith and Hope fade out of sight and only Love is left? What will it be? We cannot tell. We do not know. Only this we know: the travail of the journey is not worthy to be compared with the glory that shall be revealed to usward, even to usward, though we be the least of the redeemed.

* * *

Christ has given 'talents' to all his servants and there comes a day when his assessment of those talents will be given. In Amy's words:

> To each is given a bag of tools
> An hour glass and a book of rules,
> And each must build ere his work is done
> A stumbling block, or a stepping stone.

Her calling as a mother meant 'cutting the toe nails of a thousand children', and doing that with a greater hope in view. For numbers that hope was to be fulfilled: 'We shall train them to live for others, not self.'[33] Through the years, from the company of those once children, there have been those who have remained at Dohnavur to look after 'senior citizens', or to nurse in the hospital which at one point annually served 1,800 in-patients, and over 60, 000 out-patients, when local facilities were few.[34] Others work with different Christian agencies, or in secular employment, and 'many marry and establish Christian homes'.

Today rescue from temple prostitution in India is no longer needed but 15 million women in India are said to be still living in slavery. As a shelter for needy children Dohnavur continues its work, and with the same vision left to it by

[33] Further information from The Dohnavur Fellowship, Dohnavur, Tirunelveli District, Tamil Nadu 627 102, or from websites, www.dohnavurfellowship.org.in or www.amycarmichael.org. 'No appeal has ever been made for money, only for prayer; but many, through the years, have sent sacrificial gifts. Never has an unprotected child been refused for lack of funds: never has a patient needed to be turned away because he or she could not pay for medical help.'

[34] Hospital statistics for the year 2013–14 were 797 in-patients (including 72 leprosy) and 37,626 out-patients.

Amma, to be 'an overflowing pool of love—overflowing on others'.

Amy's 'stepping stones' were the people she guided and, through her books, readers across the world. For missionary history and devotional reading they remain near the front of evangelical literature. 'The work of a good book,' wrote A. W. Tozer, 'is to incite the reader to moral action, to turn his eyes towards God and to urge him forward.' Amy Carmichael's writings belong to that category. Numbers who took her books up only out of interest, put them down to pray.

21. Amy at her desk in her room.

7

THE BIBLE AND
WORLD EVANGELIZATION

Rationalism is that principle which asserts the supremacy of human reason in all knowledge. The Gospel, on the other hand, claims to be a communication to men, not a product of human consciousness. Its source is supernatural. It is a message from God to the world, neither discovered nor evolved by any of the processes of the natural mind. The differences between these two systems, if rightly understood, are fundamental. Rationalism excludes what the Gospel asserts. The Gospel denies what rationalism claims.

A church infected by rationalism is crippled in its mission to the world. It loses its evangelistic spirit, and if it still sends forth missionaries, they will too often be men who have only a broken evangel for non-Christian people. In a recent number of the CMS *Review*, Dr Julius Richter wrote of how the Danish-Halle Mission has been killed by this rationalism. An Indian bishop, writing last year, said: 'There is a great tendency among many of our younger missionaries, especially those working among the educated classes, to adapt the Gospel to the spirit of Hinduism, and to keep in the background the doctrines which seem to be stumbling-blocks.'

An Indian Christian, writing in *1909*, and expressing his pain at the increase of 'higher criticism' among missionaries, says: 'They help to destroy our faith rather than build it up. What is needed as far as India is concerned, is to awaken the churches of England and Scotland to a firm and solemn resolution not to send out men and women who are not faithful to the Lord and his Word.'

Notes from: *Rationalism or the Gospel? With Special Reference to Their Relative Influence on Christian Missions,*
Rev. H. E. Fox, Prebendary of St Paul's,
late Hon. Secretary of the Church Missionary Society,
(London, 1912).

Historian of Christianity in Asia, and son of American missionaries to Korea, Samuel Hugh Moffett, lectured in 2005 on 'Has Christianity failed in Asia?' Asking what made missions grow, he answered:

> The best answer I know was given by my father fifty years ago. To an inquiring committee from America, he simply said, 'For the last fifty years we lifted up to this people the Word of God, and the Holy Spirit did the rest.'

He concluded his address with convictions which were also those of Amy Carmichael. Christianity will fail, he warned, if

> Christians lose their enthusiasm for evangelism ... If they do not validate their spiritual message with social compassion and integrity ... Finally, Christians will lose everything if they abandon their theological centre: one God, Father, Son, and Holy Spirit; and one

Saviour, Jesus Christ; and one definite, inspired rule of faith and practice the Scriptures.[1]

Another son of missionaries, George Adam Smith, born in India in 1856, lived to promote a very different answer. As a minister, and then professor of theology in the Church in Scotland, he came to believe that better education had rendered traditional faith in the inerrancy of Scripture impossible, and that to continue to hold it would only hinder an acceptance of the Christian message among the intelligent. Warning was given that Smith's teaching 'seriously hindered the evangelistic work of the church', but a charge of heresy brought against him was dismissed by his denomination.[2]

Initially arising in Germany, this changed view of Scripture was not long established before it was transmitted to India. Amy Carmichael has written of her dismay when she early came across it among Brahman leaders. On a rare

[1] *Princeton Seminary Bulletin* (vol. xxvi, 2005), pp. 208, 211.

[2] I have written of this, and of the change taking place in Scotland, in *A Scottish Christian Heritage* (Edinburgh: Banner of Truth, 2006), ch. 11.

occasion when she gained access to these men in their quarters, adjacent to a famous temple, she found 'they knew a good deal about Christianity. Several had studied in Mission schools.' After speaking, there came a barrage of questions and, as she answered them from Scripture, she was suddenly interrupted,

> a voice broke in authoritatively: 'We cannot accept answers from that book. Your own Gurus are not agreed about it. Some say it is composed of legends and fables, mere myths at best. Yes', and he turned to the men, 'there are Christian scholars who say so. The book is not to be regarded as entirely true.'
>
> It was evident he had read, and somewhat misunderstood, translations of certain English articles bearing upon the inspiration of the Bible, which had begun to appear in India. One felt as if one had been hit by mistake by a shot from one's own side. I was not prepared to find this objection in a remote country town ...
>
> 'You are alone', said one at last when all the excitement had subsided, 'and you see how many we are. This is how the case stands all over India. Who will fill the highest positions

open as yet to us? Who will then rule the land, though you white rulers do not know it? Hindus! Do you think your Lord Jesus Christ will rule it?' And they laughed in scorn.[3]

Twenty years later Amy faced the possibility of a changed view of Scripture entering Dohnavur itself. I have referred above to her refusal to allow Stephen Neill to take the lead in Christian instruction when he came to the family in 1925. An important aspect of that refusal has not, however, been clarified by those who have written on her life, with the result that, in at least one case, she has been unjustly censured. In disagreement

---

[3] *Overweights of Joy*, pp. 83-6. The effect of the view that 'the Bible is a book of the highest interest, but not to be trusted as a depository of absolute truth' was noted by Canon Liddon, preaching at St Paul's Cathedral, December 22, 1889. He spoke of the indefinite message which resulted, and asked, 'What has this attenuated Christianity to say to the heathen? If a man should become a missionary on behalf of so thin a creed as this, it may be predicted he will not do much for the men to whom he addresses himself; for the heart of heathendom would say to him: "If this be all you have to bring us, why approach us at all? Why not stay at home, and leave us to make the best we can of our own twilight, without being distracted by yours?"'

with her action, Gaius Davies has written, that 'Amy's response to differences of opinion, and to friction of any kind, was to be rid of the irritant.'[4] In his view, by losing Neill, Dohnavur lost the asset of a man who would become 'the brilliant bishop of Tinnevelly'.

But the context of this episode puts Stephen Neill's dismissal in a different light. The 1920s had seen rejection of the inerrancy of Scripture carry almost all before it in England. In 1922 it caused a split in the Church Missionary Society, with a considerable number becoming the Bible Church Missionary Society. Henry Venn, nineteenth-century leader of the CMS, declared in 1842 that the hopes of the society's members rested in the maintenance of 'that scriptural, Protestant, and Evangelical tone ... the upholding of the Bible, and the Bible alone, as the foundation and rule of faith'.[5] But by 1917, when it had

---

[4] Gaius Davies, *Genius, Grief and Grace*, p. 256. For more information on Neill (1900–84), and his character, see Wikipedia.

[5] Quoted in G. W. Bromiley, *Daniel Henry Chas. Bartlett, A Memoir* (Burnham-On-Sea: Dr Bartlett's Executors, 1959), p. 20.

become widely claimed that the trustworthiness of Scripture did not extend to matters of history and science, a memorial was put before the committee of CMS asking for 'a relaxation in the orthodoxy of candidates, especially in relation to their understanding of Holy Scripture'.[6] This was the issue which would break CMS in two in 1922. Stephen Neill would later comment tersely, 'Division had struck the Evangelical cause at its most sensitive point.'[7] What exactly Neill's belief was on the issue when he left Cambridge for Dohnavur in 1925, is not recorded, but the indications are that he was already influenced by the

[6] *Ibid.*, p. 22. Further on the subject, see W. S. Hooton and J. Stafford Wright, *The First Twenty-Five Years of the Bible Churchman's Missionary Society*, (London: BCMS, 1947).

[7] Stephen Neill, *Anglicanism*, p. 400. Andrew Atherstone addresses the issue in writing on 'The Infallibility of Scripture' in *Evangelicalism & Fundamentalism*, pp 61-65. Prebendary H. E. Fox in 1920 asked all missionary societies not to send out 'any who deny or doubt that every writing of the Old and New Testaments is God-breathed, through men who spake from God, being moved by the Holy Ghost'. The CMS declined to give any such assurance. The opinion was expressed that liberal evangelicals within the Society were using a 'mutilated Bible'.

new 'understanding' of Scripture prevalent in the academic world. 'Dohnavur was a long way from Cambridge', Elliott commented, and, as already noted, the Neills believed Amy was affected by 'strong Plymouth Brethren nonconformism'.[8] But what was involved was the historic evangelical belief in Scripture; it was the belief of all the first missionaries to India, from William Carey onwards. Three years later Neill was to join the Church Missionary Society, and his later writings make clear that he belonged to what he called 'a new type of Evangelicalism', which believed the word of God 'is supremely to be found in the Holy Scriptures. But this is not the only Word of God to man.'[9] That the word of God is only found *somewhere* in Scripture is not what Scripture says of itself. Once the idea of an only partial trustworthiness in the Bible is accepted, a 'great gulf' of doubt lies open.

Some may argue that in 1925 Amy Carmichael was not in a position to make judgments involving different views of the Bible. That supposition

[8] *Chance to Die*, p. 269.
[9] Stephen Neill, *Anglicanism*, pp. 122-3.

is contradicted by what she wrote in 1913. Her life of her friend, Thomas Walker, required her to give a thorough look at all his papers and, as her biography of him included the subject of 'higher criticism' and the Bible, she had to be aware of the issue. In reference to the subject, she quoted Walker's praise of Professor Griffith Thomas for 'his strenuous and courageous championship of the old faith ... We greatly need men of this type who are firmly fixed on the Rock of the Supreme Authority of the Bible.'[10]

'Don't let us be afraid of being called old-fashioned and narrow minded,' Walker wrote, 'all the scholarship is not on the side of the critics.' But for a long time to come, the claim was to be that the intelligent were all on one side. Griffith Thomas was one of the few leaders who stood out in opposition. In 1921 he wrote a major article on 'Modernism in China', showing how the abandonment of faith in all Scripture was already prevalent on the mission field.[11] When

[10] *Walker*, p. 385. Although completed by 1913, *Walker of Tinnevelly* was not published until 1916.

[11] *Princeton Theological Review*, October 1921, pp. 630-71.

he spoke on the authority of Scripture among missionaries in China he was accused of 'driving a wedge between them'. To which he answered that the wedge was already there; and, to those who discounted the seriousness of the issue, he replied, 'the inevitable tendency of Liberalism on the Bible is to minimize the supernatural, and that the logical outcome is Rationalism.' Griffith Thomas was speaking to the same effect in England in 1922, at the time of controversy among the CMS.

Amy kept up with news from England and one cannot credit the idea that she had little or no idea of what was happening. In 1925 she had to make a stand on Scripture and, as Wellman writes, 'Certainly never again would she get people who came to Dohnavur to straighten out her mission.'[12]

The advocates of the new view of Scripture claimed that their more 'intelligent' approach to Christianity would speed its claims at home and across the world. Neill looked for 'increasing

[12] Sam Wellman, *Amy Carmichael, Selfless Servant of India* (Uhrichsville, Ohio: Barbour, 1998), p. 156.

influence in Church affairs in the coming generation'.[13] Others spoke of 'possibly the greatest missionary impetus that we have known for centuries'.[14] For Thomas Walker and Amy Carmichael such hopes were based on sand and they saw reason to fear the opposite. 'It makes one anxious about Britain's future,' Walker wrote in 1911, 'for an Empire in which religion seems to be losing its hold is in a precarious condition.'[15] It was his belief that 'a missionary famine is upon us', and he wrote to Amy from England at the same time, 'You would be terribly grieved if you went home now: you would see a great change everywhere; things seem much shallower all round.'[16]

Griffith Thomas concluded his article on China with the words,

[13] *Anglicanism*, p. 401.

[14] Quoted in Ned B. Stonehouse, *J. Gresham Machen, A Biographical Memoir* (Grand Rapids: Eerdmans, 1955), p. 473. Machen's stand against missionaries of liberal belief in China led to his own deposition from the ministry, but God had other means to remove them.

[15] *Walker*, p. 441.

[16] *Ibid.*, pp. 434-5.

Higher Critical teaching does not produce spiritual results in China any more than it does here. As an English evangelist once said, 'German theology is no use in a revival.'

Amy Carmichael's difference with Stephen Neill was no small matter. Given the general change which was taking place, and affecting many of the mission stations of the world, she was ready to accept a degree of isolation. She knew that faith in God is inseparable from faith in Scripture. While numbers were to falter, the example of her faithfulness was to see the work of Dohnavur continue down through the years to the present time. Too many Westerners drifted, and Indian nationals stood where she stood. 'Carey', write Ruth and Vishal Mangalwadi,

> spent enormous energy in translating and promoting the Bible, because ... he believed that God's revelation alone could remove superstition and inculcate a confidence in human rationality—a prerequisite for the modernization of India.[17]

[17] *William Carey, A Tribute by an Indian Woman* (New Delhi: Nivedit Good Books, 1993), p. 40.

To that belief Amy Carmichael's life and work remain a witness. 'For them that honour me I will honour, and they that despise me shall be lightly esteemed' (*1 Sam.* 2:30).

BIBLIOGRAPHY

Biographical

Frank Houghton, *Amy Carmichael of Dohnavur, The Story of a Lover and her Beloved* (1953).

Elisabeth Elliot, *A Chance to Die, The Life and Legacy of Amy Carmichael* (1987).

Sam Wellman, *Amy Carmichael, Selfless Servant of India* (Uhrichville, Ohio: Barbour,1998).

Poetry

Dohnavur Songs, for private circulation (Dohnavur Fellowship, 1959, reprint ed., 1993).

Paper Books and Selected Songs from the Wings, chiefly by Carmichael (Chennai, South India 600 005: Graphic Park, 2002).

Current, or recently current, Carmichael writings[1]

The following all published by
CLC Publications.
PO Box 1449, 701 Pennsylvania Avenue,
Fort Washington. PA 19034:

Mountain Breezes, Collected Poems of Amy Carmichael, an anthology gathered from 29 of her books (1999).

Mimosa, A True Story (1924, reprint ed., 2013).

Gold Cord, The Story of a Fellowship (1932, reprint ed., 2002).

Rose from Brier (1933, reprint ed., 2006).

Gold by Moonlight (1935, reprint ed., 2013).

Kohila (1939, reprint ed., 2001).

God's Missionary (1939, CLC, 2010).

Edges of His Ways, Selections for Daily Readings (posthumous, 1955, reprint ed., 2011).

---

[1] A full listing of Carmichael titles, as far as 1950, is given in Houghton's biography, p. 383.

Candles in the Dark, extracts from her later writings (2014).

From other publishers

Things As They Are, Mission Work in Southern India (1906, reprint ed., Read a Classic.com, 2011).

Overweights of Joy (Saraswati Press, India: 2012, and other publishers).

Film

A video/DVD, *Amma: The Story of Amy Carmichael and the Dohnavur Fellowship* is available from the UK office. See below, p. 168.

Audio CDs

Also available are two audio CDs—Vol. 1: *Beauty of Dawn* and Vol. 2: *Moonlight on the Mountains*.

Each CD contains approximately 17 or 18 songs composed by Amy Carmichael. More information about both CDs can be obtained by visiting dohnavurfellowship.org.in/amy-carmichaels-songs-cd-project/ or by contacting the Dohnavur Fellowship at the addresses on p. 168 below.

THE DOHNAVUR FELLOWSHIP
TODAY

The ministry of the Fellowship continues today on the same principles with which it was founded, and is led entirely by Christians of Indian nationality. Some changes have resulted from government decisions. The dedication of girls to temples is no longer legal. Uncared for babies have to be adopted by couples, and girls in need of a home cannot now be received at Dohnavur before the age of five and only with permission from the Child Welfare Committee. Their number today (2012) is about 119 up to the age of eighteen, and they continue to grow up in 'cottage families' under the care of an *accal* (elder sister). Other young people remain in full-time education beyond the age of eighteen. There is no longer any residential care for boys but, in the space formerly used for the boys, a co-educational boarding school, Santhosha Vidhyalaya, was opened in 1982. Initiated by the Dohnavur

Fellowship, in conjunction with other Christian agencies, this school is now administered and financed separately by the Santhosha Educational Society. Dohnavur girls go to government recognised boarding or day schools after the age of ten or eleven.

In addition to the needs of the girls, much more goes on daily at Dohnavur where more than 300 meals are prepared, three times daily, for those who are part of the community. In 2013 they numbered 337, being made up of children, staff, disabled adults and retired Indian workers. Much of the provision comes from the dairy farm, rice lands, fruit and vegetable gardens, owned and run by members of the Fellowship. The work is also supported by its own laundries, offices, workshops, builders, carpenters, needlewomen and electricians.

Besides its 70 beds, the hospital serves the needs of thousands in out-patient clinics (including dental and leprosy), with the stated aim, 'that all patients and relatives should hear the gospel'. Services are attended by numbers from different religious backgrounds.

The oversight of the work is in the hands of staff members. They are all committed Christians who form a General Body of Members. The President, at present, Sura Carunia, and other office-bearers, are elected by the members, who are also responsible for the admission of new members. The doctrinal basis is faith in the Bible as the word of God, the atoning death of the Lord Jesus Christ, and the transforming power of the Holy Spirit. Continual emphasis is given to prayer and a private prayer letter, *Dust of Gold*, is sent quarterly to those around the world who support the work in prayer. Prayer is asked 'for wisdom in bringing up children in this adverse climate and for a good rapport between us and the government officials'. The Fellowship was registered under a Juvenile Justice Act in 2010, and its validity needs to be renewed every three years.

No appeal has ever been made for money, only for prayer but many, through the years, have sent sacrificial gifts. Never has an unprotected child been refused for lack of funds: never has a patient needed to be turned away because he or she could not pay for medical help.

In the UK the Dohnavur Fellowship Corporation is a charity which has continued to support the Dohnavur Fellowship's children's home and hospital.

Addresses and Websites

Dohnavur, Tirunelveli District,
Tamil Nadu 627 102, India.

www.thedohnavurfellowship.org.in
www.amycarmichael.org

Several of Amy Carmichael's songs with musical scores are available for download.

www.archive.org for a number of early Carmichael titles.

www.proni.gov.uk for a large amount of documents.

UK Secretary:

Miss Tahany Hanna
80 Windmill Road,
Brentford,
Middlesex, TW8 0QH
Telephone & Fax (44) 020-8569-8952

OTHER BOOKS BY IAIN H. MURRAY

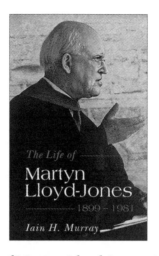

The Life of Martyn Lloyd-Jones 1899–1981
ISBN: 978 1 84871 180 8
Illustrated | 496pp. | paperback

This book is a re-cast, condensed and, in parts, re-written version of the author's two volumes *D. Martyn Lloyd-Jones: The First Forty Years* (1982) and *The Fight of Faith* (1990). Since those dates, the life of Dr Lloyd-Jones has been the subject of comment and assessment in many publications and these have been taken into account. The main purpose of this further biography, however, is to put Dr Lloyd-Jones' life before another generation in more accessible form. The big story is all here.

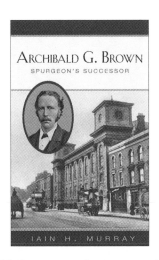

Archibald G. Brown, Spurgeon's Successor

ISBN: 978 1 84871 139 6
Illustrated | 432 pp. | clothbound

Evangelist, church-planter, and pastor amid the squalor and degradation of the notorious East End of London, Archibald Brown's life is a remarkable story of faithful and fruitful service to Christ. In an age when many were turning away from the faith, Brown stood firm and, alongside his good friend C. H. Spurgeon, saw the power of the Holy Spirit at work in the conversion and transformation of thousands of lives. Lessons for today abound in this exciting new biography of a humble yet truly great figure of the nineteenth-century church.

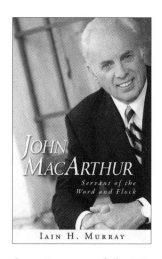

John MacArthur: Servant of the Word and Flock

ISBN: 978 1 84871 112 9
Illustrated | 264pp. | clothbound

Through more than forty years John MacArthur has opened and taught the word of God in Grace Community Church, Los Angeles. A people united to Christ, and to their pastor, has become a channel for blessing across the earth.

But his is also a human story, including the shaping of his youth, the strength of marriage and family, the refining influence of trials and controversies, and the building of a man whose staff have never known him to be angry. There are friends who, for all their love of his ministry, say his life is his best sermon.

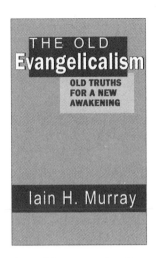

The Old Evangelicalism:
Old Truths for a New Awakening

ISBN: 978-0-85151-901-2 | 226pp. | clothbound

Sin, regeneration, justification by Christ's righteousness, the love of God as seen in the cross, assurance of salvation—these are the truths that once thrilled churches and changed nations. Yet, where evangelicalism continues to affirm these truths, without such results, it is often assumed that she must have needs that cannot be met without something new.

Iain Murray here challenges that mindset. While the Bible, not history, is the textbook in these pages, Murray draws on the best authors of the 'old evangelicalism' to confirm what a glorious message the gospel is.

The Banner of Truth Trust originated in 1957 in London. The founders believed that much of the best literature of historic Christianity had been allowed to fall into oblivion and that, under God, its recovery could well lead not only to a strengthening of the church, but to true revival.

Interdenominational in vision, this publishing work is now international, and our lists include a number of contemporary authors along with classics from the past. The translation of these books into many languages is encouraged.

A monthly magazine, *The Banner of Truth*, is also published. More information about this and all our publications can be found on our website or supplied by either of the offices below.

THE BANNER OF TRUTH TRUST

3 Murrayfield Road,
Edinburgh, EH12 6EL,
UK

PO Box 621, Carlisle,
Pennsylvania 17013,
USA

www.banneroftruth.org